MW01251638

Managing Organized Chaos™
Business Planning 1.0

Managing Organized Chaos is a series of books written to teach the fundamentals of business development, operations and management.

Business Planning 1.0 is the first in the series and focuses on writing a solid and purposeful business plan that will get your idea to the exact place you envisioned.

Managing Organized Chaos™
Business Planning 1.0

CHRISTOPHER KAIZER

www.kaizerconsulting.com

MANAGING ORGANIZED CHAOS™.
Copyright © 2011 by Christopher Kaizer
All rights reserved.
Printed in Canada

No part of this book may be used or reproduced in any manner whatsoever without written permission. For information and contact details go to www.kaizerconsulting.com.

This book may be purchased for educational, business, or sales promotional use. For information please contact us via the email address info@kaizerconsulting.com.

FIRST EDITION

Canadian Cataloging-in-Publication Data

Kaizer, Christopher
Managing Organized Chaos: Business Planning 1.0 /
Christopher Kaizer – 1st ed.
224 p. 21 cm.

ISBN 978-0-9878773-0-7

1. Business Management, 2. Entrepreneurial Success, 3. Self Help
(KP) Kaizer Publications 2012

To My Wife and My Parents

CONTENTS

CHAPTER 1

CHAPTER 8

CHAPTER 9

CHAPTER 10

ACKNOWLEDGEMENTS

I would like to thank all the people that gave me the direct support needed to complete this book. I would also like to thank those who contributed indirectly when you interacted with me sometime in my life. You see, even the most insignificant element or experience, especially those not even worthy of memory, adds to the overall wisdom gained from the many lessons of life.

To my wife Clancy, your support and love makes me a better person every day. Thank you for being a wonderful wife and mother and letting me just be me. This book would not have been possible without your understanding of who I am.

To my parents who never gave up on me and always encouraged me to believe in myself even when times looked the darkest. Having my own son was the only way to see it from your point of view and realize you were right. Well, most of the time.

To my good friend Fid for never questioning how I spend his investments and never asking for anything in return other than for me to do what I thought was right; regardless of the outcome.

To Vince who showed me that managing the darkest side of business is possible and teaching me that chaos is a good thing. You were the largest contributor to my knowledge of business management.

To my friend Gerasimos for always giving me an ear to listen and for always making it seem like I came up with the idea on my own.

And to all my past employers and clients who let me "earn while I learned" about the secrets of business management. Because the truth is; "when you stop learning, you just stop."

And to all my friends, readers and future employers who continue to support my work.

Thank you.

FOREWORD

In my life I have done an unusual amount of different and unrelated things. I worked at many completely different jobs for many different types of people. I have seen the world from nearly every perspective because I walked a lot of miles in many different shoes.

I was able to feel the softest and most expensive Versace alligator skin loafers on my bare skin; which I did not really appreciate until I got blisters from wearing no brand second (third, forth, or who knows) hand smelly thrift store Velcro ones.

I have owned the most expensive cars and could afford the most expensive of unnecessary luxuries that now make me feel sick and embarrassed when I think of the money I wasted.

But at another time, I called the service elevator of one of my employer's buildings home during the night. I showered and lifted weights for free at a friend's gym to keep up appearances. I ate all my meals "on the house" at another friends' restaurant. And oddly enough I never feel embarrassed when I think about those times; as a matter of fact I feel proud that I was able to build something from nothing and know I can do it every time I try.

I even believe that building something from nothing may be the true meaning of financial freedom. I believe this because the fear of losing something you have and not knowing if you can ever get it again is very stressful and takes all the joy out of having it. Knowing how to get it back takes that stress away and enables you to truly enjoy what you have for as long as you have it.

It has been said that we are on a roller coaster ride called life and everyone takes their turn. The cycle of life is never ending and what goes around most definitely comes back around. Markets go up and markets go down, true global economic stability won't be seen in our lifetime but individual stability is certainly possible if you possess the knowledge.

I hope you enjoy reading this book as much as I enjoyed writing it, and I hope it helps you to gain the knowledge necessary for developing something from nothing more than your vision of what could be.

Sinccrely,
C. Kaizer

DEFINITION

Managing Organized Chaos™

Verb,
The process of taking charge of, handling, or directing to bring about positive change to an entity engaged in continual activity that is, or appears to be, in disorder.

[Manage] - man•age [man-ij] (managing: engaged In the act of)
Verb
    1. To bring about or succeed in accomplishing, sometimes despite difficulty or hardship.
    2. To take charge of.
    3. To handle, direct, govern, or control by action.

[Organized] - or•gan•ized [awr-guh-nahyzd]
Adjective
    1. Having a formal organization or structure, especially to coordinate or carry out widespread activities.
Verb
    1. The combining or structuring in an organized company, party, or the like.

2. To assume organic structure: The company's systems are now organized to be one of synergistic process.

[Chaos] - cha•os [k-os]
Noun
1. Any confused, disorderly mass.
2. The behaviors of systems that follow deterministic laws but appear to be in disorder based on initial conditions; small changes in those conditions can lead to quite different outcomes.

INTRODUCTION

Anyone who has ever succeeded or failed in the attempt to start a business from scratch will agree that it is one of the hardest things to do.

I have heard time and time again from all types of people claiming to have the greatest idea ever. They feel that this idea gives them the automatic right to receive the funding and support necessary to make their vision of this idea a reality from whom ever they give the privilege of hearing it. Time and money is wasted on drafting a rock solid non-compete, non-disclosure agreement, just to tell your hardly thought out idea to anyone who will listen.

If this sounds familiar, don't feel too bad. I admit that I am also guilty of believing that one or two of my ideas were so great that everyone should stop everything they were doing and jump on board to make millions overnight.

What I have learned the hard way (hard way is not listening to wisdom from those who know) is that, yes it is technically possible for that unplanned, not structured idea to work out how you imagined; you have an extremely better chance of winning the lottery.

The hard truth is that ideas are "a dime a dozen" and everyone has them.

You need a proper vehicle to get your idea from your head to market and that vehicle is built from the wisdom and knowledge of people who have done it; more than once.

One of my mentors and good friend "Vince" once told me *"most successful non-franchised businesses succeed by mistake"*.

What he meant was that these successes usually didn't start off as businesses at all. They started off with people simply doing what they loved to do, and because they loved to do it, they did it right and almost always for free. But unfortunately it has been proven that the odds of business success occurring from this type of scenario are very, very rare.

Also unlike the rest of the world, they had plenty of free time and usually did not have to worry about paying the rent or putting food on the table.

You probably heard of a few rumored examples in your city, but some of my favorite "non-rumored real successes" are Bill Gates, Steve Jobs, Sharron Osborne and even Justin Beiber. Yes even Justin Beiber is a business and the product is: Justin Beiber.

The people I just mentioned are household names because not only did they succeed; they continue to succeed at their chosen business. And no matter how they got their initial success they could not continue without proper structure to support their business.

As an experienced professional, I can tell you that starting a business without support is *nearly* impossible. But continuing to operate that business without support is *totally* impossible.

Support means different things for different people and it presents at all different levels, but always falls under two main categories:

1) **Financial Support**
Unless you have someone paying the bills, financial support is needed to survive while you build your business' foundation. Like I mentioned before, you need to know how your idea will make you money or change the world as you imagined.

One of the major building materials in any business foundation is the business plan. The sub title of this book is "Business Planning 1.0" and will be referred to many times in these pages. A business plan can take a little while to prepare correctly and no-one is going to pay you to do one for yourself.

A business plan tells external stakeholders like bankers, customers, suppliers and future employees about the level of understanding you have about your intended venture. But <u>most</u> importantly, during the preparation of a business plan, a map has been created that gives YOU the business owner the direction to eventual success. But since most people only think of a business plan as a necessity for funding I will focus on that. A proper business plan is your key to unlocking your bankers vault providing you with the much needed financial support. Better?

2) **Knowledge Support**

Knowledge support is <u>not</u> just about the overall technical knowledge relating to the offered products and services. It is much more than just knowing how to hammer a nail or weld a pipe. An example would be a licensed tin worker, gas fitter and plumber opening a heating and ventilation business. Yes they have the technical knowledge to perform the work but lack the knowledge of planning, designing, starting, and running the actual business.

Over the years I have recommended to clients an incredible book written by Michael E. Gerber titled The E-Myth. I have one right in front of me on my book shelf. It is all about the obvious, the right in front of us, good thing it doesn't bite sort of thing. It goes into detail about why technical knowledge as the technician is not enough.

Managing Organized Chaos – Business Planning 1.0 was written as a guide to help people who want to start a business or who already own a business to understand how to properly structure that business for success. It will also help you to learn the difference between a business and performing a service and/or selling a product of that business.

If you take the time to fully read and understand each section of this book, you too will learn how to formulate a business plan that will take your idea to places you want to go. But more importantly this book will teach you how to evaluate and know if your idea is as wonderful as you thought; before telling everyone how smart you are and embarrassing yourself. Ok you got me; I'm talking about myself again.

As a business developer I have sat with many people who admit they thought they understood what it took to structure a business plan but only came to me after they realized they didn't.

By now they are frustrated, broke and ready do give up on their once life changing idea, and I was their last chance for a miracle. Talk about pressure.

For most of them it was too late, but for others it was their time to let someone else do what they now realize they couldn't. It turned out that for them to appreciate what I was doing; so they would actually follow my directions, they had to see the difference between what they did and what they should have done.

In doing so I realized that trying to find good examples of every type of individual business to show "the right way" was difficult. Other than franchised businesses each business has slightly different ingredients in their plan and caused a lot more confusion than expected, which led to a lot of frustration to me.

One of the many examples causing confusion and frustration:

When failing company A read the plan of a successful company B, company A thought company B was only successful because of one of the products they sold. Company A thought if they just sold this product they too would be a success. Long story short; company A still failed.

I needed to find the best business plan example that fit every industry. And wouldn't you know it, right there hidden in plain sight I found it on my own computer, in the file I created for my very own business plan.

My business is business development and I am a consultant for many different businesses. Every time I get a client I have to understand what it is they want to accomplish, then find out the best and most efficient way to do it.

Every business needs the same questions answered of what, how, by whom, when, where, why and etc. So what better business plan example to use than that of a business consultant?

So here we go…

Each chapter and subsequent section in this book includes a description of what is expected to be explained in your business plan. It is then followed by an altered version of the Kaizer Consulting business plan.

Business plans are not always written the same way, so you do not need to worry that it is an exact copy as long as the key elements are present in your plan.

It should also be noted, how a plan is sectioned off is a direct reflection of the writer or entity it was written for. Some sections are not applicable to some industries or individual businesses in an industry. However include all sections but place N/A or Not Applicable where not needed to show the reader that it was thought about and evaluated, not just forgotten.

Also remember that every business plan is a continual work in progress that never stops evolving. As such, your plan is only as viable as circumstances at the time of writing would allow.

So make it a habit to revisit your plan at least once a year while the business is operating, or anytime you feel improvements can be made.

CHAPTER 1

BUSINESS OVERVIEW

The business overview is a detailed description of your operations and all of the major factors that do now or will eventually affect your business. For example your business may sell small predrilled particle boards. Your sub industry may be electrical components and your main industry may be telecommunications. All of which affect your particular business.

Your industry description tells the reader exactly what your industry is as a whole. You can never assume that everyone is familiar with your industry. Since there are so many variables it must be written as though you are explaining it to someone who has never before read a business plan in their life.

When finished it must have answered the questions relating to:

- What your business produces or sells?
- How you do it?
- Where it operates from?
- What your business details are? Ex: Corporation number, business number, background, etc.

The internet is a wealth of information at your fingertips but beware of opinion sites. Other sources of information you may consider to complete this section are trade journals, newspapers, existing market and industry studies, experts and/or colleagues in your industry, etc.

For startups it is important to demonstrate your knowledge of the industry and your specific niche, and that you are aware of any difficulties of entering this field.

Examples:
- You must know how strong the existing major players are?
- Are you dependent on your suppliers or distributors? If so, explain the extent of dependence.
- You must have a good explanation as to why customers will deal with you instead of other companies offering the same products and services.

Industry Description

1. Give your company's name followed by what it does.

Ex: Kaizer Consulting is in the business of providing consulting services.

2. Describe in detail what your company does and how it's done. Ex: A consultant is a professional who sells expertise in a specific area (or areas) to clients, providing them with assessments on their practices, helping them identify problems and solutions, and advising them on possible courses of action.

Consultants act most commonly as advisers, but they may also be employed to address any other type of situation where their specific experience and knowledge is required. For instance, a consultant could be asked to implement his or her recommendations, provide training sessions on his or her area of expertise, take part in the planning of a corporation's strategy, design promotional material, evaluate bookkeeping methods, etc.

In fact, there is no activity that is exclusive to consultants or any activity from which they are expressly excluded. From branding and marketing programs to designing new packages, they are a cost-effective alternative for companies over hiring a full-time employee.

Remember: You can use all the examples given and modify them so it fits with your business. As previously mentioned, a consultant works with every type of business so large portions of the example business plan text will be relevant to most businesses.

3. It is also recommended to show the range of customers your business could service. *This is not where you list actual customers. There is a separate section for that.*

Ex: Consultants can work:
- For large consulting firms
- For boutique firms (i.e. small specialized firms)
- As independent contractors
- As contractors working within an organization where some form of employer, employee relationship already exists (this depends on the statutes and regulations of the organization, as well as its needs).

Business Details

1. In this section you need to give specifics on your company like your corporation number and when it was registered or started.

2. Give the reasons why you started it and why you feel qualified to open such a business. If you just bought a franchise, all of this information will already be included along with plenty of background and performance statistics of the company.

Ex: Kaizer Consulting was federally incorporated September 1st 2000 and offers consulting services for business and government. It is based on the owners 15+ years experience dealing with all aspects of business development as a certified project manager.

3. Include what you feel is important to the success of your business. List how you will run the business and/or demonstrate your knowledge of what it takes to succeed.

Ex: Each request from a client/customer will be treated as a temporary endeavor undertaken to create a unique product, service, or result that has a definite beginning and end.

Note: Temporary does not necessarily mean short in duration, as most projects are undertaken to create a lasting outcome.

4. Giving examples is a great way to get your point across.

One project example could be creating the proper framework for a new business. The lasting outcome for a new business is that the business will possess the tools necessary to succeed and profit if used correctly. However, most if not all projects have several smaller projects or goals that have to be met and completed along the way. Ex: The first goal might be to incorporate the company. Another may be to register a domain name similar to the company's operating name for a new website. Again another goal would be to build the website that would have even smaller goals such as: designing the logos and branding to go with the marketing, building the website's databases and shopping carts, designing proper security etc.

Projects can also have social, economic, political, and environmental impacts that far outlast the project themselves.

Ex: The benefit to Kaizer Consulting of treating each request as an individual project is repeat business within an organization and direct contacts and observers of that organization. This is because projects are undertaken at all organizational levels and can involve a single person, a single organizational unit, or multiple organizations. If the project is the development of a product that is a component of another item or an end item itself, the end of that project would be the beginning of one or more new projects. A newly produced product now needs to be marketed, manufactured, distributed, and sold which would involve several different organizations along the way.

At this point I am hoping you have a solid grasp of how to utilize this book the way I have intended. I will continue to provide as much explanation throughout as possible to make sure your business plan is rock solid.

Major demographic, economic, social and cultural factors

1. Here you need to place your business' operations and products/services in a global context. It is very important you show how your business will succeed based on demographic changes.

2. This section will help you to learn what trends will influence your company's performance in the long term and how to prepare your marketing for these changes.

Ex: _Company Name_ is located in _City Name_, the capital city of _State/Province_. _Company Name_ holds an ABC business procurement number along with a 123 membership to find all available government and private offers. _Company Name_ is currently approved for any contract up to $???,000 without having to go through a bidding process.

For contracts above the $???,000 threshold a formal bid must be submitted and awarded through a request for bid process.

3. List future goals and why those goals are important to you.

One of the company's future goals is to apply for a standing offer which will allow high dollar contracts to flow directly to the company without a formal bidding process.

4. Explain why your company will be able use its knowledge, training, tools, and background to succeed.

As stated previously, the company markets its services to business and government using project management as its foundation. Since the field of project management is globally standardized by the Project Management Institute, of which the owner is a member, Kaizer Consulting can operate anywhere with any organization.

Major players (suppliers, distributors, clients)

This section will allow you to show the level of control you have in your market and on your costs. To do this you should be able to answer the following questions.

- Who controls the market?
- Are there major players with whom you must do business?
- Are there clients who control the market due to the size of their orders?
- Who drives pricing?

1. Your business may have many different suppliers, manufactures, distributors, etc. that you will have to list.

Ex: The major player in this industry is the federal Government followed by large for-profit and not for-profit corporations, state and local governments, and then medium to small businesses.

Nature of the industry

In this section you need to describe the industry in which your business operates. As mentioned, your particular business may be affected by more than one industry. Listing multiple industries will inform the reader that your business has a greater stability potential.

The underlying purpose of this section is really about helping the business owner identify additional revenue streams for their products and services and evaluate existing ones.

Using the example listed in the Business Overview section and expanding on it, we are able to get a look at a bigger picture. The names have been changed but this example is based on a real company that I have dealt with in the past.

The example business (let's call it Kaizer Particle Boards or KPB for short) produces and distributes small predrilled particle boards to an electrical components manufacture called ECM.

If KPB exclusively sells to ECM then the future of KPB is completely dependant on ECM for life. It does not matter that the entire industry of telecommunications is growing in leaps and bounds because KPB only sells to ECM. At this time it is irrelevant who ECM sells to and here is why.

There may be multiple unidentified scenarios that could be at play here and they need to be identified and overcome.

One scenario could be that KPB was established as a separate company for the sole purpose of supplying ECM with small predrilled particle boards. If in fact KPB is a separate company this scenario does not allow any potential for growth past the volume of business provided by ECM. The bottom line is that KPB does not possess self sustainability.

In this scenario we see that KPB is completely reliant on ECM for business. But if ECM is a very well established company with a good track record and good earnings then KPB has great survivability.

Note: In reality a bank will want to know if ECM can forcibly decrease its costs to KPB. You will want to make sure you have an answer for that.

If ECM is in a volatile market with an uncertain future, KPB needs to look for other customers to sell its products to.

Trends in the industry

This section will show how your industry began, how it has performed as a whole and will give a good prediction of how it will perform in the future.

1. Identify major trends affecting your industry and your business' past, present, and future. Evaluate the opportunities and threats to your business by answering the following questions.

- How do your business' products and services fit in those trends?
- How can they be adapted?
- What is the growth rate?
- Are there any export markets?

Hint: Wikipedia should have history for most industries. Stay away from opinion blogs because they are not factual.

Example History - The first management consulting firm was founded in 1886 by the MIT professor Arthur D. Little, of the same name and was incorporated in 1909. In 1914 Edwin G. Booz was the first to serve both industry and government clients.

Example Growth - The first wave of growth in the consulting industry was triggered by the Glass-Stengel Banking Act in the 1930s, and was driven by demand for advice on finance, strategy, and organization. From the 1950s onwards, consultancies not only expanded their activities considerably in the United States but also opened offices in Europe and later in Asia and South America. After World War II, a number of new management consulting firms formed, bringing a rigorous analytical approach to the study of management and strategy.

During the 1960s and 1970s the Harvard Business School developed the tools and approaches that would define the new field of strategic management, setting the groundwork for many consulting firms to follow.

The industry experienced impressive growth in the 1980s and 1990s.

In 1983, Harvard Business School's influence on the industry continued with the founding of Monitor Group by six professors. Consulting services were gaining considerable importance in relation to national gross domestic product.

2. Don't forget to mention negative aspects. It shows that you have researched the risks also.

Ex: The industry stagnated in 2001 from the decline of the stock market. It recovered in 2003 until the economic downturn in 2009 and has now stabilized which shows that as a business service, consulting remains highly cyclical and linked to overall economic conditions.

3. Let the reader know exactly where your industry is today.

Ex: Currently, as of 2012 and looking forward, there are three main types of consulting firms.

1. Large diversified organizations;
2. Medium sized management consultancies and;
3. Boutique firms which have focused areas of consulting expertise in specific industries, functional areas, technologies, or regions of the world.

Government or other Regulations

Find out what laws, by-laws, regulations, environmental concerns, tax breaks and tax shelters for certain types of investments affect your business.

The websites of various levels of government can provide all the necessary documentation to you for free. These sites will tell you exactly to what extent your industry is regulated and how it will affect your business.

CHAPTER 2

MARKET

This section is where you give specifics about your market or region such as:

- Is your region or market different from the industry norm?
- Do you have a niche?
- Does your region present any challenges or opportunities?

Market Segment

This section is similar to trends in the industry but focuses more on your particular "piece of the pie".

Here you need to describe your specific market within your industry such as: size, region, potential, growth rate, profile, etc., and you can mention the evolution of your business while answering the following questions:

- Will you serve only one market or target many different ones?
- How will you serve them?
- Why is your service beneficial?
- Do you plan to enter different markets or serve different segments over time?
- Why these markets were chosen?
- Are you planning to export?

Examples:

Market - Consultants function as bridges for information and knowledge, and external consultants can provide these bridging services more economically than client firms themselves because they have a greater diversification of experience outside the client company.

How - Consultants have specialized on tasks that would involve high internal coordination costs for clients, such as organization-wide changes or the implementation of information technology. In addition, because of economies of scale, their focus and experience in gathering information worldwide and across different industries renders their information searches less costly than for clients.

Benefit - External consultants like Kaizer Consulting act as Virtual managers, which were brought about by the rise of the internet, globalization, outsourcing, and tele-communication. As such, Virtual Management is extremely cost effective since the manager or management teams, groups, and/or individuals rarely, if ever meet face to face.

Markets - Due to developments in information technology within the workplace, along with a need to compete globally and address competitive demands, organizations have embraced virtual management structures. Virtual teams are typically composed of team members who are not located face-to-face and their communication is mediated through information and communication technologies (e.g. video conferencing, email and intranets). Virtual teams represent an important emerging organizational structure which facilitates collaboration between team members located almost anywhere in the world.

Why – These markets have a proven demand. It is estimated that 41 million corporate employees globally will spend at least one day a week as a virtual worker, and 100 million will work from home at least one day a month.

The use of consultants to implement a virtual team structure has been shown to produce many benefits including reduced real estate expenses, increased productivity, access to global markets and even environmental benefits due to a reduction in airline flights, for example.

Virtual teams are also becoming increasingly popular with workers who want to work at home, which can increase employee engagement. Furthermore, as a result of using appropriate communication media, a virtual team is not limited to members from the same physical location or organization. As such, team members can be assembled according to the skills and backgrounds required, from anywhere in the world, enabling the organization to become more flexible and to compete globally.

Products and Services

This section is pretty straight forward. Here you need to list and explain the products and services your company offers.

You also need to show why customers will want to purchase these products and services from your company.

Note: You can include information from all sections and expand on it.

If you wish you can show competitors websites, promotional literature, trade journals, etc. to identify existing in demand products and services.

Describe how the characteristics, the positioning and the distinctive factors of your products and services will guarantee your success.

- How do your products and services compare?
- Can you improve on what the competitors offer?
- Is there a way you can differentiate your products and services from others on the market?
- Can they hold a distinctive positioning in the customers mind?

Examples:

Characteristics - As mentioned, Kaizer Consulting operates under the parameters of Project Management. This makes our products and services completely synergetic, since providing one main service usually includes several other services. The services are listed below with a description.

1.   **Business Registration** involves choosing a name by doing a name search and receiving a reservation number which is needed for the incorporation process. I prefer registering a federal numbered company since it is easy and has no wait time for name approval. Then you can register a trade name later after you find an acceptable website name, which leads to the next service:

Note: A name search and reservation is required for trademarks also.

2.   **Website Development** is mandatory to all businesses because these days if your business doesn't have an online presence, it doesn't exist.

But just having a URL does not mean you will attract potential customers. A website is part of the overall operation of your business model and is the most major part of your marketing in the 21st century.

Website development involves finding and registering a URL (website name), figuring out the best hosting plan; that alone involves determining how much data will be utilized, how many email address are needed, what type of databases are needed, what type of systems integration will be designed, setting up a proper security protocol, designing forms, determining the site layout by industry, showing the client how to use the options, setting up proper internet marketing, and the list can be endless.

3.   **Marketing** is very necessary but often overlooked when funds are tight. But before deciding to spend what funds you have on just any marketing you must first determine what type of advertizing is best for your industry.

Then you need to narrow it down based on your financial limitations and who your particular target audience is. Unfortunately, this cannot be done effectively until you know your business, and that cannot be done until you have the number one tool any business can possess: A Business Plan.

After you know where you will be marketing, there are more completely necessary steps (goals, projects) that need to be completed first such as: designing a logo that will give your company brand recognition.

Note: The logo or any other elements may have been completed already during web design or any other phase.

4.   Our **Business Plan Services** is the <u>most</u> important part of any business; yet most business owners don't realize it until it's too late.

This part may sound familiar since it is the basis for this whole book.

If you already have a business plan you know that routine maintenance is necessary to keep your company operating at optimum levels.

Your business plan is the most valuable tool you can have. A business plan is a detailed description of your business and it is a map of your business' future.

A poorly done business plan is a map to a poor future, but is still better than not having one at all. A poorly done business plan should, at the very least, have a basic layout of the business and what you want to achieve.

Note: If you cannot at least put down what your business does and what you want out of it in bullet form, you have failed before you have even begun.

With those simple details in place, and depending on the depth of detail present, there is a slightly lower learning curve for people like me to make it a good business plan; which translates to a lower cost paid out by you.

Did you notice I said "good" business plan not "perfect" business plan?

That is because there is no such thing as a perfect plan. A plan can only be theoretically perfect based on all known elements at the time of writing it. As time passes and life happens, your plan must be reviewed, evaluated and updated.

Here is proof why a business plan is so important:

According to Statistics, 80% of all businesses fail in North America (even higher for the rest of the world). That means that for every 10 people you know who own their own business, 8 will fail. The usual reason is that they are wandering in the wilderness without a map or compass to guide them. They think that if they just keep going they will eventually find civilization. Well I can guarantee that they won't. Not having a business plan is fine if you don't plan on ever really growing, ever getting a business loan or getting investors. It is also fine if you never want to sell your business or get the big customers. And it is also fine if you always want to be the one doing all the hard work.

But then why are you in business to start with if you don't want anything?

Part of business plan writing includes "Business Analysis" and is used to help us all get a preliminary understanding of a business' current strengths and weaknesses, calculate impact on profitability, and determine a course of action.

Some of the questions that need to be answered may seem basic and rudimentary, but all serve a specific purpose.

A complete list of business questions is located in Appendix B at the back of this book.

A few examples are:

Question relating to business history

- What is your industry?
- How long has your business been operating?
- Why did you start the business?
- What has your experience been so far?
- Do you have a business plan?
- Do you have documented goals?
- Have you reached any of your goals?
- Do you keep track of time spent in your business activities?
- Do you keep track of business appointments in a scheduler?
- Have you made changes to try to improve the business?

- Have you consulted with external experienced business advisors?

Questions relating to sales and marketing

- Who are your customers?
- What age group do you target?
- How do you attract customers?
- Do you get referral business?
- What marketing have you tried?
- Do you know how to analyze the outcomes of your chosen marketing?
- Do you have a marketing budget?

Questions relating to finance

- Are you profitable?
- What are your payment terms with customers?
- Do you make an effort to collect accounts receivables?
- Are you paying your bills on time?
- Do you have long term debt?
- What financial reports do you generate?
- How often?
- Do you keep copies of receipts in a filing system?

Questions relating to the management of your business

- How many employees do you have?

- How many people are in a management position?
- Are you getting the results you want from your people?
- Have you been successful in this kind of business before?
- Do you have documented standards and procedures for your people?
- Do you have training manuals?

Questions relating to your vision

- What is your vision for your company?
- What are some key challenges for your business?
- Etc…

5.   **Security Services** is both a stand alone service and part of many other services such as: web design, database management, and risk assessment.

Ex: Kaizer Consulting has licensed personnel with the ability to intellectually and physically blend in to any environment and are experienced at designing a proper Technical Security Program.

We offer:

A.   Government and Corporate Building Security set up and operation

- Optimum Camera locations / Access limitations
- Background Checks
- Loss Prevention

B. The collection of paper, photographic and video evidence in a proper manner.

- Interview/Interrogation
- Asset Locate
- Skip Tracing
- Adoption/Custody
- Labour Discrimination Wrongful Termination
- Civil Rights Violations
- Libel/Slander/Defamation
- Malpractice (Medical/Legal)
- Personal Injury such as: Automobile, Motorcycle Accident, Dog Bites, Slip and Fall, Sexual Abuse, Insurance Fraud etc...

C. Assessing threat levels

Level 5 - Includes government, military and law enforcement and involves information that is classified or restricted, of high value either nationally or internationally and may relate to national security. Corporate clients providing products or services to government, military or law enforcement are often placed at this level.

Level 4 - Includes large corporate / business and local government clients who deal with valuable confidential or proprietary information including research and development, large contract or business acquisitions, protective operations, stock or shareholder issues as well as matters of both public and media interest.

Level 3 - Includes businesses involved in matters of litigation, Labour disputes and contract bids. Others may include business plans and financial activities along with collection and storage of confidential business, customer or client information.

Level 2 - Includes matters of privacy invasion, investigative surveillance, identity theft, personal litigation and information relating to home based businesses.

Level 1 - Includes individual private information involving domestic issues such as spousal or family disputes. May also include issues or disputes with friends, neighbors or business associates both past and present and involve surveillance attempts as well as matters relating to harassment.

Note: Security and risk assessment is required for almost every business.

6. **Risk Assessment** ensures that an organization identifies and understands the risks to which it is exposed. Risk management also creates

and implements an effective plan to prevent or reduce the impact of a particular risk event.

While it is not literally possible to see the unforeseen, a good risk management plan includes strategies and techniques to recognize and confront all possible threats and determine the consequences of occurrence. This is done by asking questions which lead to more questions.

- What can go wrong?
- What are the implications?
- What will we do if it happens?
- How do we prevent it from happening?
- How do we lessen its effects?
- What is the difference between the "cost to prevent it from happening" and the "cost after it happens"?

Like traffic lights telling you when to stop and go, a good risk management plan lets you know when it is safe to proceed in business.

Kaizer Consulting has developed a Risk Assessment and Contingency Plan template for many organizations to use. It can be copied and modified to fit your business.

Instructions for the completion of a government facility/system contingency plan are provided as an example.

Beginning of Instructions

1.1 PURPOSE

The purpose of the Template is to provide a documented structure for a Facility/System contingency plan. In doing so, the completed template will provide documentation of instructional and reference information for emergency response, back-up operations, and post-disaster recovery for information technology systems and installations in the event normal information technology (IT) operations are interrupted.

1.2 SCOPE

The scope of the template is for a single facility or system within Kaizer Consulting. The Template is meant to accommodate and specifically address each critical system owned or under oversight by the Facility.

2 CONTINGENCY PLANNING

2.1 DEFINITION AND BACKGROUND

A contingency plan is a plan for emergency response, back-up operations, and disaster recovery for information technology systems and installations in the event normal operations are interrupted. The contingency plan should ensure minimal impact upon data processing operations in the event the information technology system or facility is damaged or destroyed.

2.2 NEED FOR CONTINGENCY PLANNING

Information systems operated by Kaizer Consulting are a highly essential asset in fulfilling its mission and improving service. There is always present the possibility for destructive events, both natural and man-made, which can damage or disable the information maintained and processed for core business functions and the means to access this information. By filling out this template, receiving authoritative approval, testing the plan recommendations through exercises, and keeping the plan current, Kaizer Consulting will greatly reduce the costs involved with restoring those information systems that are partially or totally destroyed from damage in a calamitous event.

3 PROCESS

The contingency planning process can be organized into three phases. The first is "Pre-Planning" and strategy development where objectives are defined, critical dependencies are determined, critical planning assumptions are made, responsibilities are defined, project management is instituted, and strategic parameters are defined.

The second phase, which is the "Planning Phase," is the actual writing of the plan. A seven step contingency process is recommended. These steps are:

- obtain commitment from executive and senior management
- establish a contingency planning working group
- perform a contingency plan capability assessment
- perform a risk assessment
- establish system priorities
- analyze and define requirements for recovery
- design the final program for contingency operations

The contingency plan, which will be developed from the template and associated Contingency Planning Working Group sessions, will primarily focus on this phase.

In the third phase, or "Post-Planning Phase," actions are carried out for testing, exercising, and training on the plan. The instructions for the scale and frequency of these activities should be contained in the contingency plan developed from the template.

The goal in providing this template is to enable independent facilities of Kaizer Consulting to complete this process more efficiently, and assure that contingency plans are written with a completeness to resolve any disaster or event that severely disrupts systems within your facility.

4 FORMAT INSTRUCTIONS

4.1 INSTRUCTION TEXT

Instruction text describes what you must consider before writing a section, and what should be in that section. You should read the instruction text, follow it, and remove it from the final Contingency Plan.

Instruction is in regular (non-italic), black Times New Roman font such as this.

4.2 EXPLANATORY TEXT

Explanatory text provides background and information on why a section is important. It may help you understand what the section should contain. It should <u>not</u> be included in the final Contingency Plan and must be removed before completion.

Explanatory text is in regular (non-italic), blue, Arial font such as this.

4.3 SUGGESTED TEXT

Suggested text may, in many cases, be used as it reads in the Contingency Plan template. You should review it to make sure that it applies to your organization's circumstances, and modify it if necessary. It is not mandatory to use it, but you may use it if you wish.

Suggested text is in italics. You should change the italic typeface to regular before including it in your Contingency Plan.

4.4 EXAMPLE TEXT

Example text shows an example of what might be written. The example may apply to another Facility/System or be hypothetical. It might be included to give you an idea of what your plan may look like, but it is unlikely that you will be able to use it as-is.

Example text is in red italics. You should remove it and replace it with your own words, normally not italicized.

4.5 COMPLETED PROGRAM PLAN TEXT

When completed, the report should be submitted in black, non-italic Times New Roman or similar font at 12-point size. All colored, italic, or Arial text that this template uses should be removed, as it is present only as an aid to the author.

End of Contingency Plan Instructions

Note: A full contingency plan example is provided and downloadable from our website:
www.kaizerconsulting.com

Human Resource Services involves implementing best practices to ensure the supply of skilled and qualified individuals and to enhance the capabilities of the current workforce; aligning with the organization's ongoing and future business plans and requirements to maximize return on investment, and secure future survival and success. Kaizer Consulting can provide: a) Full testing capabilities to ensure the potential hire possesses all the required knowledge for the position. b) Complete screening of applicants for security clearances. c) Psychological and Psychometric testing. d) Candidate interviews, etc.

Pricing and Distribution

In this section you will need to answer even more questions.

Remember - It is much better to answer the questions now and get them right instead of answering them later when asked by a customer and getting them wrong.

- What is your main pricing strategy?
- Is it higher, lower or equal to others in your industry?
- What is your distribution strategy? (networks, discounts, etc.)
- How will your customers find your products and services?
- How much will they cost?

A good idea may be to identify and list your competitor's and major player's prices and strategies first. My favorite is always to search their website, but you can also find out what the competition is up to with trade magazines, trade shows, promotional materials, etc. Then compare your prices side by side.

One well known company that really benefitted from that strategy is Geico insurance.

Examples:

Pricing - Traditionally, the consulting industry charged on a time and materials basis, billing staff consultants out based solely on the hours worked, plus out-of-pocket expenses such as travel costs.

Industry Norm - During the late 1990s and early 2000s, there was a shift to more results-based pricing, either with fixed bids for defined deliverables or some form of results-based pricing in which the firm would be paid a fraction of the value delivered.

The current trend seems to favor a hybrid with components of fixed pricing and risk-sharing by both the consulting firm and client.

Market Trends

- Is your market prone to change?

This is different from your industry. Ex: The demand for ABC products you sell will remain high, but if the people buying them are doing so at a greater rate from superstores and a lesser rate from your current distributor, your costs may increase.

Example Trends - The use of management consultancy is becoming more prevalent in non-business fields including the public sector; as the need for professional and specialist support grows, other industries such as: government, quasi-government, and not-for-profit agencies are turning to the same managerial principles which have helped the private sector for years.

An industry structural trend which arose in the early part of the 21st century was the spin-off or separation of the consulting and accounting units of the large diversified professional advisory firms most notably GHIJK & LMN, PQR and STUV. For these firms, which began operation as accounting and audit firms, management consulting was a new extension to their organization. But after a number of highly publicized scandals over accounting practices, such as the Enrap scandal, these firms began divesting their management consulting units to more easily comply with the tighter regulatory scrutiny that followed.

In some parts of the world this trend is now being reversed, where the firms are rapidly rebuilding their management consulting arms as their corporate websites clearly demonstrate.

1. Include credible studies, not opinions listed on blog sites.

Example:

Below is a portion of a study done by

> The Center for International Business
> Tuck School of Business at Dartmouth
> September 17, 2007

One large firm noted the importance of having an office presence in countries that are critical to specific industries. For example, US-based clients in the automotive industry expect their consulting firm partners to have offices in Japan. Thus, client demand for firm presence in a given geography may be based on knowledge benefits rather than on a client's intention to produce or sell in that geography. Another important consideration noted by several firms is indigenous client demand. While clients with global operations can generally be served from remote offices, it is particularly important to have an office in a country, if a firm wants to serve locally focused clients that are based in that country. In fact, one smaller firm indicated that it does not plan to expand beyond its existing office base – for example, by establishing an office in Asia – until it has sufficient additional demand from local companies in other geographies.

While client demand has historically been the main prerequisite for globalization of consulting firm operations, the existence of such demand is not, by itself, a sufficient justification for expansion abroad. The majority of firms have established screening criteria to guide decisions related to the opening of new international offices. For some firms, these criteria are laid out formally in company documents, while for others, they reside in the tacit knowledge of upper management. In aggregate, the firms ask the following questions when deciding whether to open a new office:

• Is there a critical mass of clients, in general, that can be served from the office?

• Is there a critical mass of large, global companies that are based in the country?

• Are there companies based in the country that have the potential to become large, global companies?

• Does demand for consulting services in the country appear sustainable in the long term?

• Do existing clients care whether the firm has a presence in the country?

• Will companies that are based in the new geography contribute to the firm's global knowledge base? That is, will knowledge acquired while working with companies in this new

geography be useful for other clients operating elsewhere in the world?

• Does opening a new office in the country fit with the needs and strategy of the firm as a whole? In other words, does the new location make sense when considered as part of a larger portfolio of office locations?

• Are there partners who are willing to relocate to the country to manage the office?

It is important to note that although most globalization efforts in the management consulting industry tend to be opportunistic in nature, occurring primarily in reaction to existing client demand rather than in advance of it, some firms have taken proactive steps to identify international opportunities. For example, one large firm claims that it has always invested in Asia ahead of the business, citing the opening of its Tokyo office only three years after the founding of the company in the U.S. At another firm, the executive committee regularly reviews expansion opportunities, with South Africa, the Middle East, and Eastern Europe constituting the most recent geographies under consideration.

Implications or Risk Factors

Briefly identify the strengths, weakness, opportunities and threats (SWOT) inherent to your market and show how your business will respond in a positive manner.

Example of Weakness - As with face-to-face teams, management of virtual teams is a crucial component in the effectiveness of the team. However, compared to leaders of face-to-face teams, virtual team leaders face the following difficulties:

(a) Logistical problems, including coordinating work across different time zones and physical distances;

(b) Interpersonal issues, including an ability to establish effective working relationships in the absence of frequent face-to-face communication; and technological difficulties, including appropriate technology and ease-of-use.

(c) In global virtual teams, there is the added dimension of cultural differences which impact on a virtual team's functioning.

Now add your version of **Strengths** below by using the examples given for weaknesses and modifying them. It's that simple.

Strengths - As with _____ _____ _____ _____ is a crucial component in _____- _____. This is where our strengths and

advantages come from. Compared to _____
_____, …

(a) Logistical advancements, including _____,
gives us _____etc…

(b) Our ability to establish effective working
relationships in the absence of_____
and

You get the point.

Planned Response

Determine your major product and market strategies
in terms of products and services, pricing,
distribution and communications (advertizing,
promotion, direct marketing, etc.), and assess your
business' future performance in the market. Take
the weaknesses mentioned and say how you plan to
respond in a positive way.

Note: These represent your overall corporate
strategies.

CHAPTER 3

COMPETITION

In this section, identify and analyze major competitors (direct and/or indirect) for each product and service your business offers. Determine their strengths and weaknesses (market position if known, image, size, quality, etc.) and identify your competitive advantages. Ex: The reason a customer will buy from you.

Competitors and Type of Competition

Indentify your competitors which offer similar products and services as you. Is the competition based on service, quality, pricing, distribution, etc.? Determine the elements on which your business will have to fight its way into your market or against foreign companies. Evaluate the level of competition by segment (intense, weak) and your business' market entry potential in local or in foreign markets.

Example of Possible Competition:

1. Accenture
2. Avanade
3. Aon Consulting
4. Gartner Consulting
5. Deloitte Consulting
6. Earnest and Young
7. SAIC
8. Fujitsu Consulting
9. Hay Group
10. Hill and Knowlton
11. KPMG consulting
12. Mercer Consulting
13. Oliver Wyman
14. Unisys Consulting
15. Navigant Consulting
16. PriceWaterhouseCoopers

Added to these are the many corporations that set up their own internal consulting groups, hiring internal management consultants either from within the corporation or from external firms' employees. Many corporations have internal groups of as many as 25 to 30 full-time consultants.

Internal consulting groups are often formed around a number of practice areas, commonly including: organizational development, process management, information technology, design services, training, and development.

Competitors' Strengths and Weaknesses

Evaluate your major competitors' strengths and weaknesses in various ways: quality of products and service, price (to the customer, commissions paid to the trade/distributors, production costs), products and services (characteristics in relation to needs, technology used), personnel (number, level, training, etc.), distribution (network, location, type of distribution), communications (image, advertizing budgets, visibility, media used), promotion (merchandising, trade terms, etc.).

For each competitor, gather information on its size, location, number of employees, products sold, network used, pricing and promotional activities.

Examples:

Potential Strength of Competition:

• From Corporations with Internal Consultants

There are several potential strengths of internal consultants:

1. If properly managed and empowered, internal consults can evaluate projects in light of the corporation's strategic and tactical objectives.

2. Often, the internal consultant requires less ramp up time on a project due to familiarity with the

corporation, and is able to guide a project through to implementation, a step that would be more costly if an external consultant were used.

3. Internal relationship provides opportunities to keep certain corporate information private.

4. It is likely that the time and materials cost of internal consultants is significantly less than external consultants operating in the same capacity. Note: Corporations need to be very conscious of and consistent with how internal consultant costs are accounted for on both a project and organizational level to evaluate cost effectiveness.

5. Internal consulting positions can be used to recruit and develop potential senior managers of the organization.

6. Internal consultants are often uniquely suited to either lead external consulting project teams, or act as organizational subject matter experts 'embedded' with external consulting teams under the direction of organizational management.

7. A group of internal consultants can closely monitor and work with external consulting firms. This can sometimes ensure better delivery, quality, and overall operating relationships.

8. Clients may feel external firms providing consulting services have a different priority because the health of the external firm is more important

than that of their client (though, of course, the health of their client has a direct impact on their own health).

Potential Weaknesses of Competition

1. The internal consultant may not bring the objectivity to the consulting relationship that an external firm can.

2. An internal consultant also may not bring to the table best practices from other corporations. A way to mitigate this issue is to recruit experience into the group and/or proactively provide diverse training to internal consultants. But in the long run as the recruited external consultant becomes an internal one; more recruiting is needed which defeats the purpose.

3. Also where the consulting industry is strong and consulting compensation high, it can be difficult to recruit candidates.

4. It is often difficult to accurately measure the true costs and benefits of an internal consulting group.

5. When financial times get tough, internal consulting groups that have not effectively demonstrated economic value (costs vs. benefits) are likely to face size reductions or reassignment.

Competitive Advantages

- What are your company's strengths that will help you take advantage of your competitors' weaknesses?
- What strengths will give you a chance to deal with the industry's threats to seize business opportunities that arise?

Determine the elements your business can use to distinguish itself from the other players in the industry to gain market share and profits; these will be related to the key factors developed earlier in the planned response section.

Example Advantage - Traditionally within most competitors' firms, consultants may be hired on a permanent basis which contributes to higher operating costs. Kaizer Consulting has a large competitive advantage over other firms because of the near zero perpetual operating costs. As discussed the company operates as a virtual manager and employs subcontractors only when needed. No out of pocket expenses will be laid out since our subcontracting pay agreement is modified to reflect payment after our client or customer pays Kaizer Consulting.

This, therefore, has the direct cost savings to the client without sacrificing quality.

CHAPTER 4

SALES & MARKETING PLAN

Describe your customers by name or market segment served. These customers can be major distributors with which your business has distribution agreements or manufactures that use your products and services. The customer described here would account for the majority of your business' sales; potential customers should also be included, but be realistic. Be sure to consider foreign markets and their importance to your business.

Customers

For Startups
List any customers you want to attract, and why they may buy from you. Make sure to get permission before you list them if they say they may use your company. List the reasons why they may use you in the future by contacting them and

asking them how satisfied they are with your competitor or competitors. Don't worry if they say that their level of satisfaction is so great switching would never be an option. That becomes your opportunity to ask them why? Those reasons now become the criteria for your business to implement to keep future customers as loyal to you, as this company is to your competitor.

Established companies need to list current and past customers as long as it does not violate any privacy policies.

Terms – Products and Services

What are the current or planned sales terms and conditions offered to your customer for your products and services? (terms of payment such as credit card policies, etc.)

Examples:

Billing
As with the service industry, *BLANK Co.* will charge on a time and materials basis, billing staff out based solely on the hours worked plus out-of-pocket expenses such as travel costs.

Potential Billing Options
The best payment scenario for any company, including *BLANK Co.,* would be to have full payment upfront with an option to reevaluate for a higher amount if pricing fell below what was

originally quoted. But a good payment scenario for both *BLANK Co.* and the client would be a hybrid one. It would contain the components of fixed pricing and risk-sharing by both *BLANK Co.* and the client.

Different Billing for Different Customers
The Government prefers to have results-based pricing, either with fixed bids for defined deliverables or some form of results-based pricing in which the firm would be paid a fraction of the value delivered. Fortunately the government does have amendment legislation where the prices can be adjusted upwards incase the quoted price does fall below the actual price.

Additional Product Information

Include information such as customers' expectations, special services required, cross-selling opportunities, and their development projects.

Cross-selling
In business, cross-selling is the sale of additional products or services to the same customer to increase sales. It is also associated with up-selling.

Ex: Kaizer Consulting provides many services, all interrelated, so cross-selling is as easy as listing the lacking elements of a client's business. The client recognizes the need for the product or service but decides who is awarded the sale based on the cost quoted and ease of integration over another company not familiar with the whole picture. Usually the learning curve associated with bringing in another company is what helps secure the sale to Kaizer Consulting and is, therefore, what will help our company increase profits when cross-selling.

So many additional forms of revenue can be secured from current customers. It is also much easier to keep an existing customer than find a new one. For this reason you must make sure that your customers are always treated right.

Important Note: Treating the customer right does not mean letting them walk all over you. As soon as you let them know it is alright to take advantage of you, it will happen every time. To prevent this from happening you need to be honest and make sure your contracts are detailed so everyone knows what is expected <u>upfront</u> before anything changes hands. If your customer goes back on their written word, you don't want them as a customer and neither will anyone else.

To finish up this section you need to find out:

- Is there potential for alliances or long-term agreements?
- Buy-outs or mergers? (Can your company buy out or merge with a company that already has a loyal customer base?)
- Joint marketing?

Example: Say Kaizer Consulting has a sub-contractor who specializes in web-design but has customers who need risk management services which they cannot provide, by signing an exclusive contract that entitles the sub-contractor to all the web-design work at a reduced rate to Kaizer Consulting, the sub-contractor in return gives us all their risk management business.

This has several benefits to Kaizer Consulting such as: ensuring Kaizer Consulting always has someone to perform web-design work, saving costs to Kaizer Consulting thanks to a reduced rate, and guaranteeing a steady flow of additional revenue in the form of risk management business.

The benefits to the sub-contractor are: guaranteeing a steady flow of revenue in the form of web design work, lowering costs associated with marketing to new customers, and being able to increase their overall value with services offered.

Example of Joint Marketing: As mentioned previously, giving a sub-contractor an exclusive to your web-design business means that when you advertize, they indirectly advertize and vice versa.

Suppliers (Subcontracted Consultants)

Who are the major suppliers that serve your business, and what are the terms and conditions? If you are in a highly competitive sector, it is preferable to have more than one supplier; you will be able to negotiate better prices, and will not be overly dependent on a single company or person. These suppliers would account for a major portion of your expenses, and your business success is highly dependent on them. Potential suppliers can also be included, depending on the interest their products and services represent for your business' operations.

Example:
After a client details what services are required and a partial payment is made, Kaizer Consulting hires available subcontractors as needed. Provided there are no continual business arrangements already in place with a certain sub-contractor, each subcontractor will be contracted on a performance basis, paid only after the successful completion of their duties.

All subcontractors and independent contractors are required to understand and comply with all rules, regulations, policies and procedures contained in the Ethics, Rules, and Regulations Manual provided upon initial hire.

Additional Supplier Information

It is a good idea to answer the following questions:

- How and why did you choose these suppliers?
- What advantages do they give your business?
- Do they have new products planned?
- Are they changing any pricing policies?

- Is there potential for integration?
- Have you evaluated their capacity to match your development, service new locations, or support your new products?

Advertizing and Promotion

This section will be under constant scrutiny from management because what you decide here will directly affect the future of the business. Since there is a limited budget set out for cost of goods sold, it is imperative you think your advertizing through.

Some of the contents here have already been discussed in the Market section. Here you can discuss other possible avenues.

Note: Intermediaries can also represent an important target for your communications efforts. This is where you can include details about any online efforts, creation of a website etc.

Questions that need answering here are:

Q - Are you going to advertise your products and services?

Q - If so, where and how often?

A – Example:
Yes, Kaizer Consulting will advertize to various levels of Government and private businesses both directly and indirectly. The advertizing will be done

on a given timetable (daily, weekly, monthly, etc.) basis to get the name of our company in front of as many potential customers as possible.

The direct approach will involve the use of the available contact information provided by the ABC. This contact information lists emails and phone numbers of key persons in every department responsible for offering contracts to suppliers like Kaizer Consulting.

The indirect approach to ABC but also the direct approach to DEF, will involve the use of the available contact information of DEF companies who have been awarded contracts in the past. This contact information will be used to contact other consulting firms offering the same types of services as Kaizer Consulting.

Kaizer Consulting will offer to complete a certain portion of their contracted work that they may need outsourced. (Remember the web-design company needed someone to perform their risk management services?)

Since all phone numbers, email addresses and details on a particular business, department or agency was provided, Kaizer Consulting can make an informed decision as to whom to target the marketing efforts.

Q - What is your advertizing and promotional strategy, and the main communication tools you plan to use to reach each segment or market identified?

A – The information provided by ABC relating to bids is a large portion of our advertizing; however, IBC-123 provides additional contact information and details of businesses not listed in the already provided contact details.

The entire advertizing plan revolves around a completely free, but proven method for this industry; and that is a proper internet and email campaign.

Customer Service Policy

Here you will define the service levels you intend to offer, and relate them to their costs to what your customers expect and to what the competitors offer. If you like, you can refer back to the terms of products and services section under cross-selling. I mentioned that you need to detail every contract upfront before exchanging any item with a customer.

Example: If you don't offer refunds on products after 30 days, you need to make sure the customer knows that upfront. Otherwise in 45 days when he/she calls you to say something doesn't work, you won't look bad when you say "you should have called us 15 days ago".

Some of the items you may want to include in your customer service policy are:

- Are you going to try to compete on service and quality?
- If so, what are the standards?
- How are you going to measure your customers' satisfaction?
- Will you have an 800 line or a website for information on your products or for after-sales service?
- Will it be in-house or outsourced?
- Do sales representatives also handle customer service?
- What are your after-sales service terms?
- Guarantees?
- How will you handle complaints?

Please feel free to use the provided customer service policy as a guide for your own.

Beginning of Customer Service Policy Statement

1. Our Mission
The mission of Kaizer Consulting is to provide our customers/clients with the most advantageous and cost effective solution to their needs within the individual limitations presented.

2. Our Commitment

In fulfilling our mission, Kaizer Consulting strives at all times to provide its goods and services in a way that respects the dignity and independence of people with disabilities. We are also committed to giving people with disabilities the same opportunity to access our goods and services and allowing them to benefit from the same services, in the same place and in a similar way as other customers.

3. Providing Goods and Services to People with Disabilities

Kaizer Consulting is committed to excellence in serving all customers including people with disabilities and we will carry out our functions and responsibilities in the following areas:

3.1 Communication

We will communicate with people with disabilities in ways that take into account their disability.

We will train staff who communicate with customers on how to interact and communicate with people with various types of disabilities.

3.2 Telephone Services

We are committed to providing fully accessible telephone service to our customers. We will train staff to communicate with customers over the telephone in clear and plain language and to speak clearly and slowly.

If telephone communication is not suitable to their communication needs or is not available; we will offer to communicate with customers by other means of communication that apply, e.g. e-mail, TTY, relay services.

3.3 Assistive Devices

We are committed to serving people with disabilities who use assistive devices to obtain, use or benefit from our services. We will ensure that our staff is trained and familiar with various assistive devices that may be used by customers with disabilities while accessing our services.

We will also ensure that staff knows how to use the following assistive devices available on our premises for customers.

3.4 Billing

We are committed to providing accessible invoices to all of our customers. For this reason, invoices will be provided in the following formats upon request: hard copy, large print, e-mail, etc.

We will answer any questions customers may have about the content of the invoice in person, by telephone or e-mail.

3.5 Ethics, Rules and Regulations Policy

All our employees, subcontractors, partners, and affiliates will adhere to Kaizer Consulting's strict Ethics, Rules and Regulations policy.

4. Use of Service Animals and Support Persons

We are committed to welcoming people with disabilities who are accompanied by a service animal on the parts of our premises that are open to the public, and other third parties. We will also ensure that all staff, volunteers and others dealing with the public are properly trained in how to interact with people with disabilities who are accompanied by a service animal.

We are committed to welcoming people with disabilities who are accompanied by a support person. Any person with a disability who is accompanied by a support person will be allowed to enter Kaizer Consulting's premises with his or her support person. At no time will a person with a disability who is accompanied by a support person be prevented from having access to his or her support person while on our premises.

5. Notice of Temporary Disruption

Kaizer Consulting will provide customers with notice in the event of a planned or unexpected disruption in the facilities or services usually used by people with disabilities. This notice will include information about the reason for the disruption, its anticipated duration, and a description of alternative facilities or services, if available.

The notice will be placed at all public entrances and service counters on our premises.

6. Training for Staff

Kaizer Consulting will provide training to all employees, volunteers and others who deal with the public, or other third parties on their behalf, and all those who are involved in the development and approvals of customer service policies, practices and procedures. Individuals in the following positions will be trained: customer service representatives, sales associates, managers etc.

This training will be provided as needed after staff commences their duties.

Training will include the following:

•The purposes of the Accessibility for Ontarians with Disabilities Act 2005 and the requirements of the customer service standard

•How to interact and communicate with people with various types of disabilities

•How to interact with people with disabilities who use an assistive device, or require the assistance of a service animal or a support person

•How to use TTY, wheelchair lifts, etc., available on provider's premises, or otherwise, that may help with the provision of goods or services to people with disabilities.

•What to do if a person with a disability is having difficulty in accessing Kaizer Consulting's goods and services

•Kaizer Consulting's policies, practices and procedures relating to the customer service standard.

Applicable staff will be trained on policies, practices and procedures that affect the way goods and services are provided to people with disabilities. Staff will also be trained on an ongoing basis when changes are made to these policies, practices and procedures.

7. Feedback Process

The ultimate goal of Kaizer Consulting is to meet and surpass customer expectations while serving all customers including those with disabilities. Comments on our services regarding how well those expectations are being met are welcome and appreciated.

Feedback regarding the way Kaizer Consulting provides goods and services to people with disabilities can be made by e-mail, regular post, verbally, or by telephone. All feedback will be directed to the president of the company. Customers can expect to hear back within 48 hours.

Complaints will be addressed according to complaint categories already established in our company's complaint management procedures.

8. Modifications to This or Other Policies

We are committed to developing customer service policies that respect and promote the dignity and independence of people with disabilities. Therefore, no changes will be made to this policy before considering the impact on people with disabilities.

Any policy of Kaizer Consulting that does not respect and promote the dignity and independence of people with disabilities will be modified or removed.

9. Questions About This Policy

This policy exists to achieve service excellence to customers with disabilities. If anyone has a question about the policy, or if the purpose of a policy is not understood, an explanation should be provided by, or referred to, the president of Kaizer Consulting.

End of Customer Service Policy Statement

CHAPTER 5

OPERATING PLAN

Describe the site of your business in terms of its location/s, size and capacity, advantages and disadvantages of a particular facility or location, and ownership or leasing details. You should cover current and future use and if applicable, cover all aspects of your business' production, distribution and selling activities.

Location

Ex: The major advantage to operating a business in today's technology based environment is "*Location, Location, and Location*". Where that "Location" is anywhere you have access to a computer and telephone.

Kaizer Consulting is in the business of streamlining business function and efficiency so leading by example is the best way to show our discipline.

Size and Capacity

Consider the flow of goods, people, clients, etc and impacts on space assigned, layout and size. If applicable, give details of the size and capacity devoted to the different activities:

- Production
- Warehousing for raw materials and semi-finished products
- Distribution
- Selling
- Customer service and administration

This section will vary greatly for different businesses. For Kaizer Consulting the size and capacity is determined by the project parameters at the time.

Advantages or Disadvantages

- Why was this location chosen?
- Is there extra capacity?
- Is it easy to deliver or get deliveries?
- Is it close to clients, suppliers or competitors?

Advantages - The major advantage to operating as a virtual manager using subcontractors is that we can operate our business from anywhere in the world. Kaizer Consulting can take on any project at any time. We choose who to hire as a subcontractor based on a specific skill set to best suit a particular project. Some of the advantages to this method are; local language speaking subcontractors who have area specific knowledge of regulations, laws, and already established business relationships.

Disadvantages - A major disadvantage can be finding available qualified candidates.

Lease or Ownership Details

If applicable, describe either the lease or ownership details on a site location basis (if multiple sites). Consider the impact on costs and on your operational requirements. Evaluate location/s on a long term basis. Ex: compared to the foreseen development of your business or the evolution of your market.

- Are you close to your market and to major transportation networks (access, ease for delivery, visibility, etc.)?
- Is your location appropriate to your current and future needs?
- Is it appropriate to the sales and production levels?
- To customer services?
- When and why would you need to move?

Equipment, furniture and fixtures

Describe the equipment you use to produce your goods or services.

- What is the age and remaining useful life of your equipment?
- What is the capacity and volume?
- What is the condition and replacement cost?

Depending on your type of business, the budgets and the technology, this can vary greatly.

Ex: A retail operation will need more furniture and fixtures.

Ex: Manufacturing will require more expensive equipment and technology.

For Manufactures: Manufactures should consider layouts, flow of people and goods, service vs. production vs. delivery areas, and so on. Describe the work processes, key activities and resources (equipment, machinery, furniture, vehicles and technology) necessary to operate your business as well as ball park capital expenditures and technology required for the coming years in order to achieve sales targets.

For Startups: You will need to describe the equipment you want to use. Find out what your competitors use and discuss your needs with the suppliers of that equipment, furniture and technology to determine an optimal operating plan that you can describe briefly.

Ex: The best tool Kaizer Consulting has is the knowledge and experience in all services offered. Every other piece of equipment is completely expendable and replaceable.

Future Expenditures / Technology Requirements

If you have a long term plan for equipment or technology acquisition, give the details here. Include the timeframe, reasons (ex: to maintain sales objectives) and costs. Mention the technical aspects, potential suppliers, buying criteria, alliances and partnerships, costs, etc.

These are decisions related to your long term investments and will have to be taken into account in your financial plan. Consider the impact of your sales and marketing plan and any increase in personnel or space required If there are any potential tax breaks or shelters, mention them here.

Ex: Near future expenditures for Kaizer Consulting will be for direct marketing costs that are over and above email campaigns. Currently there are no technology requirements in need of updating.

Research and Development

Here you will need to mention if there are any research and development activities. They can be in-house or outsourced and must identify the resources involved (human, material, financial).

You want to mention if there are there any R&D plans (output, dates, expected results). Also explain what the financial implications are and the long-term advantages to your business. Don't forget to mention potential effects of the R&D on any subsidiaries or partnerships that you may have.

Knowledge based industries that rely heavily on R&D will want to go into more detail in this section.

Research and development is sometimes hard to recognize and you may be doing it without even knowing.

Q - So why would you even want to know if you are doing R&D?

A - Because there are several tax incentives including tax free money that can be given to you from the government for performing R&D.

In Canada you can find the information at the following address:

http://www.cra-arc.gc.ca/txcrdt/sred-rsde/menu-eng.html

There you will find the following description of what the scientific research and development program is all about.

"The SR&ED program is a federal tax incentive program, administered by the Canada Revenue Agency (CRA) that encourages Canadian businesses of all sizes, and in all sectors to conduct research and development (R&D) in Canada. It is the largest single source of federal government support for industrial R&D."

"The SR&ED program gives claimants cash refunds and/or tax credits for their expenditures on eligible R&D work done in Canada."

"Claimants can apply for SR&ED investment tax credits for expenditures such as wages, materials, machinery, equipment, overhead, and SR&ED contracts."

According the Canada Revenue Agency you are doing scientific research and development and are eligible for a refund if what you are doing will lead to a new or an improved and/or technologically advanced product or process.

An example might be finding a longer burning candle wax to use in the candles you sell.

The great thing is there are multiple benefits at work here. The first is in the production of a product that is potentially better than your competition that could eventually gain your company a greater market share.

The second way you will benefit is when the government gives you money just for doing it.

Guess what!? Even if you fail you are still eligible providing you followed all the rules.

A third benefit is to the customer who will not have to change his candles as often.

Note: This is one of those times you need to listen to experience and not learn the hard way; as I did.

The first time I utilized the SR&ED program I did not benefit as much as I could have. Although the forms and instruction were all available to me I did not have someone to guide me through it.

Before you begin you must make sure you understand how to make your processes match the criteria listed.

Environmental Compliance

If applicable to your industry, explain in detail how you will deal with waste and other environmental issues (policies, criteria, supervision and contingency plans).

- Will you require some environmental standards from your suppliers?
- Will you offer them to your customers?

For Startups: Banks often have strict requirements when lending to companies whose activities have an impact on the environment. You will want to develop your own code of conduct; determine criteria to follow and establish "What if" scenarios.

CHAPTER 6

HUMAN RESOURCE PLAN

This section of the business plan can not be fully completed until you have figured out nearly everything else. As you go through the plan you will be putting down preliminary job functions necessary to implement each portion of your plan.

Example:
During the products and services section you will figure out:

- How your products are produced and by whom?
- Who will provide the services you offer?
- Who will do the sales of those products offered by your company?
- Who will manage the books?
- Etc.

Then based on necessity or financial limitations (identified from the completion of your Financial Plan) you will add or subtract employees.

Key Employees

Describe your employees' key job positions, both present and future. A solid human resources plan is as essential as your marketing or financial plan. Include key responsibilities, titles, hierarchical levels and the number of people required.

Note: This section is for employees; the principals of the company (president, treasurer, etc.) are described in the executive summary.

Job Title/ Key Responsibilities/ Qualifications

Describe the title, responsibilities and qualifications or skills you will require for each function. These can help you establish your recruiting and promoting criteria.

One main thing you need to know about hiring:

1. If you are planning on having your business be dependant on certain employees being able to figure things out on their own, you are already in big trouble.

We see this all the time in the classified section of the newspaper. "ABC Co. is looking for a highly motivated self starter that can work independently with little direction." Usually this involves a commission or a draw towards commission. What this ad tells me is the company that is hiring wants someone to figure out how to make their own money then split it with the company. Conclusion: If the employee was able to that all on his own he would have his own company.

A company needs to hire people that follow your (the visionaries) direction. If you have completed all the sections in this book and followed the directions set out, this train of though won't even be an issue.

You can use an organizational chart like the one included to list job functions required under a section.

Example:
COO will have an Executive Assistant (title) who is responsible for: drafting memos, arranging meetings, organizing files and other. The Executive Assistant will be required to have expert knowledge of Excel, Word, Power Point, and must type 100 words a minute for dictation.

Additional information

Don't forget to include information on external support needed in the future: lawyers, consultants, ISO specialists, accounting firm, etc. You can also attach the resumes of key people at the end of your plan.

If you are a sole proprietor working alone you are more than welcome to list your name under all of the headings.

Some title examples:
COO - Chief Operations Officer
CFO - Chief Financial Officer is usually an accountant or anyone who handles the finances of the company.
V.P. - Vice President

Main Organizational Chart example

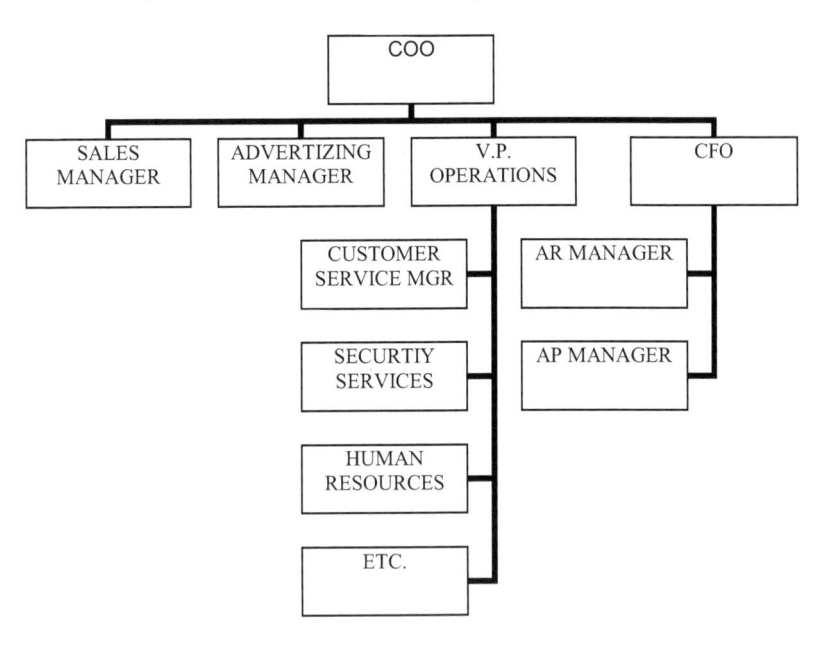

CHAPTER 7

POLICIES & PROCEDURES

In this section, describe your overall human resource strategy and include the following elements:

- Remuneration (pay, commissions, bonuses, etc.)
- Training (Remember when I mentioned all employees need follow your Direction? This is where it starts.)
- Performance Assessment

This section forms the basis of the "Contract" between management and personnel. These policies and procedures will help you attract and keep employees and achieve a work environment conducive to top level performance. Employees need direction from you to complete even the smallest task. By putting it in writing you can manage all your employees with nothing more than a reprinted copy of your directions.

Decisions here will have a direct impact on operating expenses and consequently on profits, so I have included an almost exact version of the Kaizer Consulting Ethics, Rules and Regulations document. It is provided to all employees and subcontractors.

Since it is a very long and very important part of a business plan, (also a mandatory element to a successful business) the inclusion of it here greatly reduces your learning curve. Writing one for the first time is a very daunting task and usually ends up incomplete. Please feel free to use it as a guide for your own business.

Beginning of Ethics, Rules and Regulations document.

Contents

1) Requirements
2) Regulation
A. Professional Ethics
B. Consultant Status
- B-1 Becoming a Consultant
- B-2 Legal Age
- B-3 Corporations, Partnerships and/or Trusts
- B-4 Fictitious/Assumed Names
- B-5 Consultant/Independent Consultant
- B-6 Indemnity

1) Requirements

The terms "Independent Consultant" and "Consultant" shall mean the same. As an independent consultant and/or sub-contractor of Kaizer Consulting you are required to understand

and comply with all rules, regulations, policies and procedures contained in your [Working with Kaizer Consulting Manual] which may be amended from time to time as needed.

2) Regulation

Kaizer Consulting honors all federal, provincial, and local regulations governing marketing, and requires every independent consultant to do the same. It is, therefore, very important that you read and understand the information in this section. If you have any questions regarding any rule or policy, seek an answer from our Department of Ethics and Compliance.

A. Professional Ethics

As an independent consultant of Kaizer Consulting, I hereby promise and agree that:

A-1 I will be honest and fair in all my dealings while acting as an independent consultant of Kaizer Consulting.

A-2 I will be courteous and respect the time and privacy of the people I am in contact with directly or indirectly in the course of my business.

A-3 I will perform all my professional activities in a manner, which will enhance my reputation and the reputation of Kaizer Consulting.

A-4 I will not engage in any deceptive or illegal practice.

A-5 I will not make claims for Kaizer Consulting programs, services, or products except as contained in official company literature. I also understand and agree that the responsibility of "commercial speech" claims made in the promotion of commercial goods and services exceed the requirements of either scientific, research, or other forms of "free speech". Therefore, I will remember that even my personal experience of benefits received from Kaizer Consulting services, and products may be interpreted as an "extension of labeling claims" if I use those experiences as sales advise.

A-6 I will fulfill any leadership responsibilities as a consultant, including training and otherwise supporting Kaizer Consulting.

A-7 I will make no income claims or representations regarding any compensation plan. I understand that a consultant's success depends on many variables, such as, amount of time and effort committed to his/her business and organizational ability.

A-8 I understand and agree that I am solely responsible for all financial and/or legal obligations incurred by me in the course of my business as an independent consultant of Kaizer Consulting. I understand that I am an independent consultant for all federal, provincial and local tax purposes. This includes (but is not limited to) programs, services and products including all applicable taxes, licensing fees, etc.

A-9 I will compete aggressively but fairly. I will respect other professionals who are affiliated with Kaizer Consulting. Under no circumstance will I recruit a person, company, client, customer, prospect or contact for my own purposes, regardless of whether I had previous knowledge or acquaintance.

B. Consultant Status

B-1 Becoming a Consultant
An applicant becomes an independent consultant of Kaizer consulting when:
- They have completed the required application form titled Kaizer Consulting Application Form.
- And after it has been approved by the recruiting department of Kaizer Consulting. *Kaizer Consulting reserves the right to decline any application.*

B-2 Legal Age
All consultants must be of legal age in the area of their residence and possess the appropriate certifications and/or knowledge base required to complete their duties.

B-3 Corporations, Partnerships and/or Trusts
Corporations, partnerships and/or trusts may be signed as independent consultants of Kaizer Consulting only after the approval of the Kaizer Consulting application form which must include;

notarized copies of the articles of incorporation, partnership agreement or trust documents. To ensure compliance to the Rules and Regulations, applicants must disclose a complete list of all directors, officers, shareholders, and partners. A Trust must disclose the trustee and beneficiaries. SIN/SSN numbers for each person must also be given. Shareholders, partners, beneficiaries, and trustees, directors and officers, as applicable, agree to remain personally liable to Kaizer Consulting and bound by the rules and regulation.

B-4 Fictitious/Assumed Names

A person or entity may not apply as a consultant using a fictitious or assumed name, except as a business entity.

B-5 Consultant/Independent Consultant

All independent consultants of Kaizer Consulting are strictly prohibited from stating or implying, whether orally or in writing that they are franchisees, joint ventures, partners, employees, or agents of Kaizer Consulting. Consultants have no authority to bind Kaizer Consulting to any obligation, or to speak on behalf of Kaizer Consulting, its shareholders, directors, officers, or employees.

B-6 Indemnity

Each and every consultant agrees to indemnify and hold harmless Kaizer Consulting, its shareholders, employees, agents, general/limited partners, and successors in interest from and against any claim, demand, liability, loss, cost, or expense, including but not limited to, attorney's fees, arising or alleged to arise in connection with the Kaizer Consulting business, its affiliates' activities, and any other matter related to consultant's performance under the consultant agreement.

B-7 Other Products and Services
Independent consultants of Kaizer Consulting are not restricted from working for other companies but are bound by the Kaizer Consulting confidentiality standards set out.

B-8 Taxation
Consultants will be treated as independent contractors for all tax purposes.

C. Recruiting and Training; Terms of Termination

C-1 Recruiting
Independent consultants are entitled to recruit other consultants that may be of benefit to Kaizer Consulting. However, possible recruits must follow the exact same procedures for becoming an independent consultant of Kaizer Consulting.

C-2 Training
All independent consultants will take any training or instruction Kaizer Consulting requests.

C-3 Voluntary Termination

A consultant may voluntarily terminate his/her consultant status by sending written notice to Kaizer Consulting recruiting department and receiving confirmation of arrival of said notice. Voluntary termination is effective upon receipt and confirmation of arrival of such notice by Kaizer Consulting.

C-4 Involuntary Termination

An independent consultant may be terminated or suspended for materially violating the terms of his/her independent consultant application and agreement, for failing to meet or maintain the Kaizer Consulting code of professional ethics, or for violating any of the rules and regulations. Kaizer Consulting may suspend the consultant status of a violating consultant while serving notice of cause, citing instance/s of the violation/s. Should satisfactory explanation, defense, or remedy not be provided by the consultant within 15 days, termination will become effective upon final decision notice. The decision will be sent by certified mail to the violating consultant's address of record and a copy will be sent via email to the consultants email address. In instances where applicable governing law is inconsistent with the foregoing, such procedure shall be automatically amended for compliance.

C-5 Appeal

An involuntarily terminated consultant may appeal the termination by submitting a letter of appeal, stating the grounds of the appeal. This letter must be sent certified mail return receipt requested accepting signature required and must be received within fifteen (15) days of the date of mailing of the company's termination notice. If the company has not received a letter of appeal by that deadline, the involuntary termination shall automatically become final. If a consultant files a timely appeal, Kaizer Consulting will in its sole discretion, review and reconsider the termination and notify the consultant of its decision. The decision of Kaizer Consulting shall be final and subject to no further review. If the appeal is denied, the termination shall remain in effect as of the date of the company's original termination notice.

C-6 Effect of Suspension

Should Kaizer Consulting deem it necessary to suspend an independent consultant, such suspension could mean that the consultant may not have the right to represent him/herself as a consultant of Kaizer Consulting and that any payment due will be held in abeyance by Kaizer Consulting pending resolution.

C-7 Effect of Termination

In the event a consultant is involuntarily terminated, effective with such termination the consultant loses his rights to any of his/her payment or benefits due.

C-8 Assignment

An approved independent consultant may assign, or transfer all of, or a portion of his/her contracted obligation to another approved consultant if it is deemed necessary provided notice is given, including reason/s for assignment, and approved in writing by Kaizer Consulting. The approved consultant who agrees to the assignment must adhere to all particulars of the obligation assigned including but not limited to: timelines, quality of work, and payment terms. If it is determined that such assignment was made in an effort to circumvent compliance with any agreement, rules and regulation, or compensation agreement the transfer shall be declared null and void. If necessary, and in Kaizer Consulting's sole discretion, appropriate action, including termination, may be taken against the parties involved to ensure compliance with any agreement or rule and regulation.

C-9 Succession

Notwithstanding any other provision of this section, upon death of a consultant, Kaizer Consulting shall pass to his/her successors in interest as provided by law. However Kaizer Consulting will not recognize such a transfer until the successor in interest has submitted an application and succession agreement form together with certified copies of the death certificate and will, trust, or other instrument. The successor shall thereafter be entitled to all rights and subject to all the obligations of the consultant prior to death.

C-10 Confidentiality

Information provided to a consultant by Kaizer Consulting is proprietary and confidential to Kaizer

Consulting, and is transmitted to the consultant in strictest confidence. The consultant agrees that he or she will not disclose any such information to any third party directly or indirectly, nor use the information to compete with Kaizer Consulting or for any purpose other than promoting Kaizer Consulting. The consultant and Kaizer Consulting agree that, but for this agreement of confidentiality and non-disclosure, Kaizer Consulting would not provide the information to the consultant. Any consultant who is found, or reported to be, in violation of this rule may not only be at risk of possible suspension/termination, but Kaizer Consulting may seek remedy for damages to the fullest extent that the law makes available.

C-10a Kaizer Consulting's business relationships with its vendors, manufactures, suppliers, faculty, or any other person or party is confidential. A consultant shall not contact, directly or indirectly, or speak to, or communicate with any representative or any supplier, manufacturer, faculty, or any other person or party of Kaizer Consulting except as a Kaizer Consulting consultant as it relates to a necessary component of work to benefit Kaizer Consulting.

D. Intellectual Property

D-1 The name Kaizer Consulting and any of the logos, names, phrases, and writings used by Kaizer Consulting are owned by Kaizer Consulting. Only

Kaizer Consulting is authorized to produce and market products, services, and literature under these trademarks, copyrights, patents, or trade secrets. This includes but is not limited to slides, overheads, brochures, videos, and other training and/or marketing materials and all promotional materials such as but not limited to T-shirts, caps, pins, etc. Use of Kaizer Consulting name on any item not produced or authorized by Kaizer Consulting is prohibited.

D-2 Consultants are not permitted to use any of the Kaizer Consulting trademarks, logos, etc. in any advertizing such as, but not limited to, telephone number, fax number, website, and email address unless approved by Kaizer Consulting and is for the sole benefit of Kaizer Consulting.

D-3 Consultants are not permitted to advertize or list their "800" number under the Kaizer Consulting name without submitting a request for approval and adhering to the rules of such approval.

D-4 Independent consultants are not permitted to create their own business card/s or letterhead graphics that include any of Kaizer Consulting logos, trademarks, or other material. All business cards or letterhead must be supplied by Kaizer Consulting and owned by Kaizer Consulting at all time.

D-5 Only official Kaizer Consulting literature may be used in representing Kaizer Consulting products or services. Company literature may not be duplicated or reprinted without prior written approval from Kaizer Consulting. Banners, trade show materials, and other related promotional material, must be approved in advance and in writing by Kaizer Consulting.

D-6 Only company approved materials may be used in the placement of any advertising in any print or electronic media. No person shall use Kaizer Consulting name, logos, trademarks, or other material in any advertizing not produced by Kaizer Consulting or without express written permission from Kaizer Consulting.

D-7 Media
Consultants are prohibited from granting radio, television, newspaper, tabloid, or magazine interviews, or using public appearance, public speaking engagements, or making any type of statement to the public media to publicize Kaizer Consulting, its products and services, or their individual Kaizer Consulting business except with the express, prior written approval of Kaizer Consulting. All media contact and inquiries must be coordinated through the approval and representation of Kaizer Consulting media representative.

D-8 Endorsement
No endorsements by any Kaizer Consulting officers or administrators or third parties may be alleged for any reason (ex: advertizing, recruiting, etc.) except

as expressly communicated in official Kaizer Consulting literature and communications.

D-9 Consultants, as independent consultants, are encouraged to distribute information and direction to their respected clients. Kaizer Consulting encourages the prudent distribution of official newsletters and advertizing material.

D-10 Kaizer Consulting provides commission to any consultant who generates new business (as outlined in E-2) for Kaizer Consulting in addition to your contracted obligations as a result of the newly generated business.

D-11 Consultants may not re-package Kaizer Consulting programming, information, materials, or products in any way. However, consultants may videotape and/or audiotape Kaizer Consulting programming for their personal use. This privilege extends ONLY to broadcast programming and does not include audio or video material produced for marketing and/or training by Kaizer Consulting. Under no circumstances may broadcast programming taped for personal use be distributed in any way.

D-12 Recordings
Consultants shall not produce or reproduce for sale or personal use Kaizer consulting produced audio or video taped material detailing Kaizer Consulting program/s, services, presentations, events, or speeches, including conference calls. Video and/or

audio taping of Kaizer Consulting meetings or conferences is strictly prohibited. Still photography is allowable at the discretion of the meeting host.

D-13 Consultants may not answer the telephone by saying Kaizer Consulting, or in any other manner that would lead the caller to believe that he or she has reached the corporate offices of Kaizer Consulting.

D-14 Liability
Violation of any of the rules explained in this section, as with all other sections of these rules and regulations, is grounds for termination. Kaizer Consulting may seek injunctive relief or damages from the violator for the unauthorized use of Kaizer Consulting material.

E. Payment, Bonuses and Commissions

E-1 Payment
A consultant of Kaizer Consulting is paid as agreed in their Kaizer Consulting Independent Contractors Work Agreement, along with all of the contractor's obligational requirements.

E-2 Bonuses and Commissions
Bonuses and Commissions are earned on new business to Kaizer Consulting. Business means; Kaizer Consulting is contracted to provide a product and/or service for an agreed upon fee. New business means; the successful contracting of a new

customer not already having a prior relationship to Kaizer Consulting. Consultants or others who gain new business for Kaizer Consulting cannot be paid any negotiated bonuses or commissions on new business until that customer has fulfilled the payment portion of the contract.

E-3 The payment method to the consultant from Kaizer Consulting will always be by company check.

E-4 If a customer of Kaizer Consulting fails to pay for services rendered under contract for reasons caused by the contractor such as but not limited to; failing to perform one or more duties as outlined in the Kaizer Consulting Independent Contractors Work Agreement, failing to perform the work with such due care and quality as specified, or failing to deliver completed work on schedule, then the contractor will not be paid until remedied.

E-5 If the customer of Kaizer Consulting fails to pay for services rendered that was no fault of the contractor then the contractor will still be paid the agreed rate of pay including any commissions and bonuses due. If it is found that the consultant had prior knowledge that the client was not going to pay and did not inform Kaizer Consulting then the consultant will not be paid any due amount and will be suspended or terminated.

1. General Provisions

1-1 Liability

To the extent permitted by law, Kaizer Consulting shall not be held liable for, and the consultant releases Kaizer Consulting from, and waives all claims for any loss of profits, indirect, direct, special or consequential damages or any other loss incurred or suffered by consultant as a result of (a) the breach by consultant of the agreement and/or the terms and conditions of the rules and regulations and policies and procedures, (b) the operation of consultant's business, (c) any incorrect or wrong data or information provided by the consultant, or (d) the failure to provide any information or data necessary for Kaizer Consulting to operate its business, including without limitation, the acceptance of consultant into a working relationship with Kaizer Consulting.

1-2 Claims

No consultant may give false or misleading claims or projections, including those based solely on mathematical formulation or "ideal projections" to past, current, and/or future customers, of future benefits received from Kaizer Consulting services or products. Nor may independent consultants of Kaizer Consulting represent their own incomes as indications of the success assured to other consultants or customers, since income success has many variables.

1-3 Consultants may not solicit media attention or respond to media inquiry on behalf of Kaizer Consulting, nor are any independent consultants authorized to give personal testimonials of Kaizer Consulting to the media, except as authorized by Kaizer Consulting in writing. All media inquiries should be immediately referred to the attention of Kaizer Consulting publicist and media representative.

1-4 Although Kaizer Consulting is approved as a government contractor with a government procurement business number, no federal or government agency endorses the products or services provided by Kaizer Consulting directly or indirectly. Therefore, no consultant may represent or imply, directly or indirectly, that the products and services have been endorsed by any governmental agency, unless approved in advance and used as a reference only by a particular agency.

1-5 Amendments

Kaizer Consulting reserves the right to amend the rules and regulations set forth herein, its pricing, products and services, or any other information as it deems appropriate. Amendments will be communicated to all consultants through official Kaizer Consulting publications or other means. Amendments are effective and binding on all consultants as of the date of issuance.

1-6 Non-Waiver Provision

No failure of Kaizer Consulting to exercise any power under these rules and regulations or to insist upon strict compliance by a consultant with any obligation or provision herein, and no custom practice of the parties at variance with these rules and regulations, shall constitute a waiver of Kaizer Consulting's right to demand exact compliance with these rules and regulations. Waiver by Kaizer Consulting can be affected only in writing by an authorized officer of the company. Kaizer Consulting's waiver of any particular default by a consultant shall not affect or impair Kaizer Consulting's rights with respect to any subsequent default, nor shall it affect in any way the rights or obligations of any other consultant. Nor shall any delay or omission by Kaizer Consulting to exercise any right arising from default affect or impair Kaizer Consulting's rights as to that or any subsequent default.

1-7 Arbitration

1   This agreement is performable in *City, State* and governed by the laws of the *Province/State*. The consultant understands and agrees that all claims and disputes relating to this agreement, the rights and obligations of the parties or any other claims or causes of actions relating to the performance of either party under this agreement shall be settled totally and finally by arbitration in the city of Ottawa, Ontario. The arbitrators may not award costs, expenses and attorney's fees, as each party agrees that they will be responsible for their own. The parties agree to waive any claim for punitive or tort damages, as a result of this agreement or the actions of either party. In the event litigation is necessary to seek ratification or the arbitrator's

award, the parties agree that venue lies in *City, State*. The parties hereby knowingly, voluntarily and intentionally waive any and all rights to a trial by jury, including but limited to, any claims with this agreement, the obligations referred to herein, or any course of dealing, statements {whether oral or written} or actions.

2   Notwithstanding, the foregoing, the arbitrator shall have no jurisdiction over disputes relating to the ownership, validity or registration or any mark or other intellectual property or proprietary confidential information of Kaizer Consulting without Kaizer Consulting giving prior written consent. Kaizer Consulting may see any applicable remedy in any applicable forum with respect to these disputes and with respect to money owing to Kaizer Consulting. In addition to monetary damages, Kaizer Consulting may obtain injunctive relief against a consultant for any violation of the agreement, and for any violation or misuse of Kaizer Consulting logo, copyright or confidential information policies.

3   Nothing in this rule shall prevent Kaizer Consulting from applying to and obtaining from any court having jurisdiction a writ of attachment, a temporary injunction, preliminary injunction and/or other injunction or emergency relief available to safeguard and protect Kaizer Consulting interest prior to the filing of or during or following any arbitration or other

proceeding or pending the handing down of a decision or award in connection with any arbitration or other proceeding.

4 The existence of any claim or cause of action of an independent consultant against Kaizer Consulting, whether predicated on the consultant agreement or otherwise, shall not constitute a defense to Kaizer Consulting for the enforcement of one or more items in an independent consultant covenants and agreements contained in the consultant agreement or rules and regulations.

1-8 Entire Agreement
This statement of rules and regulations is incorporated into the consultant application and agreement and constitutes the entire agreement of the parties regarding their business relationship.

1-9 Severability
If under any applicable and binding law or rule of any applicable jurisdiction, any provision of the agreement, including these rules and regulations, or any specification, standard or operating procedure which Kaizer Consulting has prescribed is held to be invalid or unenforceable, Kaizer Consulting shall have the right to modify the invalid or unenforceable provision, specification, standard or operating procedure or any portion thereof to the extent required to be valid and enforceable. The independent consultant shall be bound by any such

modification. The modification will be effective only in the jurisdiction in which it is required.

1-10 Limitation of Damages

To the extent permitted by law, Kaizer Consulting and its affiliates, officers, directors, employees and other representatives shall not be liable for, and the independent consultant hereby releases the foregoing from, and waives any claim for loss or profit, incidental, special, consequential or exemplary damages which may arise out of any claim whatsoever relating to Kaizer Consulting's performance, non-performance, act or omission with respect to the business relationship or other matters between the consultant and Kaizer Consulting whether sounding in contract, tort or strict liability. Furthermore, it is agreed that any damage to the consultant shall not exceed, and is hereby expressly limited to, the amount of payment owing.

End of Ethics, Rules and Regulations

Hours of operation

List the business hours for all functions and locations. This can help you determine the level of service required by your clients and establish a schedule for employees. There might be variations based on function (customer service vs. administration), on seasonality of demand

(Christmas period) or other factors directly related to your industry or market served.

Vacation program

Describe policies based on the level of service described above, the functions and industry/regional standards.

Training and development

Assess current level of competence, set targets and establish training programs to reach targets. The qualifications and skills identified in the Human Resource Plan should be the starting point.

For Startups: It is a good idea to show that you have both a short-term (when you start) and a long-term training plan for your employees.

As outlined in section C. of Kaizer Consulting Policies and Procedures.

C-2 Training
All independent consultants will take any training or instruction Kaizer Consulting requests.

Remuneration and benefits

For each function and hierarchical level, list salary levels and benefits packages, including fringe benefits and related programs.

As outlined in section E. of Kaizer Consulting Policies and Procedures.

E-1 Payment

A consultant of Kaizer Consulting is paid as agreed in their Kaizer Consulting Independent Contractors Work Agreement, along with all of the contractor's obligational requirements.

E-2 Bonuses and Commissions

Bonuses and Commissions are earned on new business to Kaizer Consulting. Business means; Kaizer Consulting is contracted to provide a product and/or service for an agreed upon fee. New business means; the successful contracting of a new customer not already having a prior relationship to Kaizer Consulting. Consultants or others who gain new business for Kaizer Consulting cannot be paid any negotiated bonuses or commissions on new business until that customer has fulfilled the payment portion of the contract.

E-3 *The payment method to the consultant from Kaizer Consulting will always be by company check.*

Performance assessment

All companies need to establish evaluation processes: management expectations, corporate objectives, expected results by function and hierarchical levels, qualitative and quantitative factors and impacts on remuneration and promotion.

Example: For each service or project completed, Kaizer Consulting sends a survey to the customer for input. This survey will be sent by email unless otherwise stated by customer. The results of this survey will directly reflect the performance of the subcontractor.

Please feel free to use the following as an example to create your own customer satisfaction questionnaire.

Kaizer
CONSULTING

Customer Satisfaction Survey

1. Were you happy with the service you received from Kaizer Consulting?

☐Yes ☐No

2. How satisfied were you with the overall outcome?

☐Not Satisfied at all   ☐Somewhat Satisfied

☐Very Satisfied

3. Do you feel that you were treated with dignity and respect?

☐Yes ☐No

---

4. Would you use Kaizer Consulting again in the future?

☐Yes ☐No

5. Would you refer us to others you may know who need our services?

☐Yes ☐No

6. Were there any areas that you feel we may need to improve on?

☐Yes ☐No   If Yes please explain

7. Additional comments are always appreciated.

Thank you very much for taking the time to complete this survey and helping us improve our services to you.

Health and Safety

While it may not be necessary to include a section about health and safety in your particular plan, ensuring that your company complies with legislation is a good idea. For more information refer to the Centre for Occupational Health and Safety in your country.

CHAPTER 8

ACTION PLAN

An action plan is a chronological list of your company's activities. It gives your banker and/or future partners an overview of how you intend to reach the sales levels described in your financial plan. Many of these activities and/or goals will come directly from the plans established in the prior sections. Be as precise as possible (what to do, when, by whom, how, with what objective and for what budget).

Note: When listing goals make sure that you only list **SMART** goals which are defined as:

S - Specific
M- Measureable
A - Achievable
R - Realistic
T - Time limited

Beginning of Action Plan
Example Goals:

1- Incorporate business
2- Get a business number (BN)
3- Design the website
4- Get business procurement number
5- Preparing a business plan
6- Design marketing plan
7- Advertize
8- Gain customers
9- Grow business

Purpose of goal number:

1- Incorporating the business is the formal registration of the business. It gives the business official life. Registration is necessary to accomplish step 2.
2- A business number and tax number are used to differentiate you from other businesses.
3- A website is what gives the company life on the net. In today's business environment a company that does not have a website does not really exist. It is where the general public finds about your company and is what your marketing plan is based.
4- A business procurement number or BPN is a unique identifier based on your BN. It is used to do business with government and is only issued after you complete a screening process.

CHRISTOPHER KAIZER

5- During the preparation of a business plan all aspects of the business are evaluated. Since every section must be completed, a reintroduction or reeducation of sorts is done by the owner.

6- Designing the marketing plan is crucial to the success of the business. The name of the game here is biggest bang for the buck. Kaizer Consulting is focused almost completely on internet and email marketing campaigns.

7- Advertizing is the act of implementing your marketing plan. Evaluation of your advertizing results is the evolution of your marketing plan.

8- Gaining customers is the goal of every business. Getting customers for Kaizer Consulting is all about the numbers; number of emails sent = number of emails received = number of responses = number of leads – number of contracts.

9- Growing the business is the inevitable result of gaining customers. But only if you keep them and get more.

Status / steps / timing / cost of achieving goal number:

1- Completed / filed paperwork online with government / took XX minutes because it was a numbered company that did not need a name search and reservation. Cost was $??? In fees and approximately $?? in time.

2- Completed and received automatically 72 hours after completing goal 1.

3- Completed / purchased domain name and hosting platform, set up the pages from a basic design having the main pages: home, about-us, contact-us, services, etc. Wrote information for each page including products and services. Programmed and designed databases and forms to be sent to the designed secure databases and email for backup, designed email templates for internet marketing. Time: 3 weeks. **Note:** A website is always evolving and changing. Cost $?? out of pocket expense and approximately $??,000 in time.

4- Completed application in XX minutes and received BPN 72 hours later. Could not apply until BN was received. Cost $0 out of pocket and approximately $?? in time.

5- Completed / 3 weeks (but like the website, a business plan is an ever evolving process. Cost $? out of pocket and approximately $??,000 in time.

6- Completed during the preparation of business plan (never stops evolving). $0 out of pocket.

7- Implementing the marketing plan will begin November 15th. A newly designed email campaign will be sent out to all of the addresses and contacts provided from ABC. These include public contacts as well as private contacts. This first advertizing campaign will continue every week on Mondays.

8- Since all business advertizing is based on the numbers of viewers, we expect that within 1 month we will have our first customer from this one advertizing method.

9- Growing the business is a direct result of customers gained.

Total confirmed cost to completing first 6 goals: $??,???.00

Obstacles and responses to goal number:

1- No obstacles were expected and none were presented.

2- No obstacles were expected and none were presented.

3- No obstacles were expected but some did present in the hosting platform as it related to non compatible programming languages. They were quickly resolved.

4- The expected obstacles were in the form of being denied approval of a PBN from the government. However this was not a problem what so ever.

5- No obstacles were expected and none were presented.

6- No obstacles were expected and none were presented.

7- The expected obstacles will be again due to programming uncertainties. Will the recipients email filter reject the email, send it to spam, or if it does get to the proper inbox folder will the logos be visible? The response: since most spam filters do not filter personal emails, Kaizer Consulting will be using Gmail to send the ads. Gmail is a personal email account with the capabilities to send from your business account. Meaning the spam filters will see a personal email allowing it to enter the inbox but the reader will see info@kaizerconsulting.com instead of personal account information.

8- Goal number eight is dependant on the success of goal number 7. If the emails make it to the recipient enough times statistics show if recipient is interested in the services provided (which we already know they are) a response is inevitable.

End of Action Plan

CHAPTER 9

FINANCIAL PLAN

If the business plan as a whole is the body of any business, then the financial plan is most definitely the heart. It is what keeps the blood flowing to the brain and all other organs.

Continuing with this analogy of a living breathing business plan, I will tell you with the utmost certainty that investors will examine this section first (Executive Summary excluded). If it appears that a health issue exists with the heart, an investor won't bother doing any other tests.

The financial plan is the last section of a business plan only as an aid to the writer, not the reader. All other sections must be known by the writer before attempting to make any forecasts or assumptions in the financial plan.

As stated, the reader (investor, banker) will always go to this section first, and if he or she does not like what they are reading, will never take the time to hear any of your explanations as to why you believe your numbers to be accurate.

Now with that said, you will also never be able to please every investor you approach; but need to make sure the financial plan is inviting enough for all of them to want to ask you questions. This is where you, not your plan, will amaze them with your knowledge of the business strategies that you learned while writing your plan.

Sometimes the timing of the approach is all it takes for a so called "flawless plan" to be rejected. An investor is best to approach at his year end. He will need to either offset capital gains which will be accomplished by investing with you, he may need to use any left over budgeted capital not already used during the year, or he will need to compile future investments to prepare a budget for his/her new fiscal year.

Just like the business plan, marketing plan, action plan, risk plan and every other plan, there are mandatory sections that need to be completed. I have included these sections with instructions to guide you in the preparation of your financial plan.

Section 1 - Company Information

Just like before in the business overview section, you will need to list your company details. You may be tired of imputing the same details over and over again but remember that an investor may only read one or two sections of (or even just small portions of a section) your plan before making a preliminary decision. You don't have the luxury of telling him/her that you listed certain details somewhere else. You need to make certain accommodations for him/her, not the other way around.

These details are:

1. Legal Name:
2. Trading Name:
3. Address:
4. Phone:
5. Email:
6. Form of Company:

The form of Company is just simply how it was formed. Below are 4 different types of companies:

- Proprietorship – Simplest form of business which offers relatively low start-up costs and few regulations. Beware; you are personally responsible for all debts and obligations.

- Partnership (LLP, LP) – Each partner shares in the profits, the losses and all the obligations; requires a partnership and/or shareholders agreement.

- Corporation – A legal entity, with more regulations, higher startup costs, and usually higher taxes. However, the shareholders of a corporation have limited responsibility for the debts and obligations of the company.

- Co-operative (Association) – A corporation controlled by its members.

7. Status: (Start-up, new - less than one year old, in business for more than one year)
8. Start date: (Month and Year)
9. Planned first year end: (Month and Year)
10. Last interim statement: (Month and Year)
11. Industry Sector: (main sectors listed below)

- Accommodation/Food sector
- Administrative and support
- Agriculture, forestry, fishing and hunting
- Arts and entertainment, recreation
- Construction
- Educational services
- Finance and insurance
- Health care / social assistance
- Information
- Management of Companies
- Manufacturing
- Mining
- Other services
- Professional, scientific, and technical services
- Public administration
- Real estate and leasing

- Retail trade
- Transportation and warehousing
- Utilities
- Waste management / remediation services
- Wholesale trade
- Other

12. NAICS Code: (North American Industry Classification System)
13. Percentage of sales that go to export

Section 2 - Sales

Under sales activities, enter the products and/or services you will sell. Most companies list only one or two but can list many categories. This is not an individual product or service list but a logical division of your product mix. It might help to divide them by source of revenue, product line, production method, etc. instead of actual products and services.

Note: Kaizer Consulting offers many services but lists its sales activities under Business Services.

Example: If your company is in the Food Sector and you choose to list by product line, it may be called "Spreads" for example. This line would include all products that are spreads like; strawberry jam, apricot jam, peanut butter, garlic butter, etc.

Example: Sale Activities:
Line 1) _SPREADS_____

Line 2) _____

Line 3) _____

Establish the expected sales of this line for the next 3 years using the strategies and activities you set out in your sales and marketing plan. If you are already in operations, you will need to provide the sales levels for the past 3 years to help you set your future projected sales levels.

Detail the assumptions you have been using to formulate your projections. For example, if your sales targets assume an increase of 20%, you need to indicate the reason. Example: The 20% increase is due to a planned promotional campaign. This is how the reader and, more importantly, YOU will be able to verify the accuracy and realism of your projections.

It is always a good idea to seek the advice from your accountant or experienced professional when developing a financial plan. Just remember that you need to understand everything he/she does so you can explain it intelligently and confidently when relaying it to your readers.

Ensure that all of the decisions made in the previous sections appear in your financial plan. An obvious example would be the advertizing costs outlined, but a not so obvious one would be the time it takes to advertize for, talk to and interview potential employees. In today's world everything has a cost. I bet it even cost the chicken a fee, or pavement tax, to cross the road.

Historical

Use your financial (audited if possible) statements to fill out this section.

Example: Sales activities for SPREADS

	NOV 09 /	NOV 10 /	NOV 11
1)	$15k	$19k	$23.5k
2)			
3)			

Assumptions – use this section to comment on and explain the financial evolution of your business using percentage of growth, ratios, etc. Explain why negative or positive things have happened to your business and what their impact has had on your financial results.

Describe from your historical data the elements on which you rely for your future projections.

Projected

Based on your sales and marketing, human resources and operating plans, forecast the evolution of your business over the next three years. This is where the results of your plan and actions are seen.

Example: Sales activities for SPREADS

	NOV 12 /	NOV 13 /	NOV 14
1)	$29k	$36k	$48k
2)			

3) _____ / _____ / _____

The assumptions you make are critical to these projected figures. It is at this level that you may have to generate different versions of your plan that reflect the different sales and costs scenarios.

Remember contingency planning?

Assumptions – your projected figures will be based on two key elements: your sales objectives and the costs of your planned activities.

Some costs like purchased equipment and sales estimates based on orders known in advance from a good client can be done easily. Use real figures as much as possible.

Often you will have to hypothesize or make assumptions based on the following information:

1. Historical information:
Example: The trend in revenues will continue based on average annual growth rate of last three years as seen below.

NOV 2009 - $15,000
NOV 2010 - $19,000
NOV 2011 - $23,500

2. Adjusted historical information:
Example: The last 3 years saw a smaller increase in growth compared to the future projected 3 years

because we decided to pay off the entire amount of our high interest loans. Moving forward debt free will enable us to increase production by purchasing glassware in greater quantity and lowering total per unit material costs.

Other examples: Last year's large increase in growth was because of market conditions affected by lowered regulation, or because of the launch of our newest product etc.

3. Ratios:
Example: Our industry specific ratios are X % so our company will be in line...

4. Comparison:
Example: Our company intends to follow the evolution of company Y which is the closest competitor and has earnings of ...

5. Market data:
Example: The market will grow at a rate of X based on consumer index numbers found...

Example 2: Our revenues will grow at a rate of X because we expect to gain an X % market share from the launch of our new product...

Remember, in order for your assumptions to be credible they must be relevant, which means you will need to evaluate their strength.

Startups will need assumptions that explain the sales forecasts since these forecasts are not based on actual numbers generated by your business. It may be easier to use a bottom-up method. This is done by determining the expected sales for each of your products within each region and adding them up. You can use the market size you established earlier to test your figures.

Section 3 - Cost of Sales

Also called cost of goods sold (COGS) or variable costs since they vary with production levels. (If sales increase, production increases and material costs decrease)

These are the costs incurred to generate a sale. For a production or manufacturing business these are: material costs such as inventory and raw materials, direct labor costs, repair and maintenance costs for machinery, utilities, and so on. For service businesses this section includes costs related to personnel, utilities and taxes.

You can use a constant cost of sales ratio over time based on past performance or industry norms. This ratio tends to be quite steady over the years, but can lower with productivity gains.

	Historical	Projected
Opening Inventory	_____	____
Material Purchases	_____	

Freight & Duty _____
Other _____
Closing Inventory (-) _____
Total Material Costs ($) =

Direct Labor Wages _____
Repairs & Maintenance _____
Services / Utilities _____
Depreciation _____
Overhead _____
Other _____
Total Cost of Sales ($) =

Section 4 - Expenses

With the exception of costs related to production and sales, these are the fixed costs of running a business and is usually a lump sum.

These costs include management and office salaries, as opposed to direct labor costs affecting costs of goods sold, professional fees (lawyers, accountants, etc.), telecommunications, office supplies, insurance and taxes, advertizing & promotion, depreciation, bank charges, interest payments on loans and bad debt incurred by your business.

Factors that can affect these expenses include:

- The purchase of new equipment has an impact on interest paid on long term debt.
- New administrative employees

- Expenses related to regulation and compliance issues
- New software

In the same format you will need to list all the expenses with the historical and projected data to get your total sales expenses in dollars.

Then list all administrative expenses with historical and projected data to get your total admin expenses in dollars plus any R&D expenses. Add this total to the total you already got from sale expenses to get your Total Expenses in dollars.

Don't worry if this sounds confusing, it is. Without looking at the template I created, I could never remember all this information. When it is in front of you it will all come together.

All forms and templates are available for download from our website. www.kaizerconsulting.com

Section 5 - Income Statement

You should enter other income or special expenses not included in the prior sections. From this information, and the sales, cost of goods sold and expenses entered previously, you will be able to obtain very accurate numbers for your income statement.

Depending on the results, you may want to create different scenarios or change certain assumptions, then save each plan under different scenario names ranging from the best case to the worst case. The average of these different scenarios will be the most accurate.

Based on other tested estimates, you should be in a position to estimate the following:

- Other income such as: revenues from interest and asset disposition
- Taxes, both current and deferred using current federal, state and provincial rates
- Depreciation expenses that are based on a percentage of the asset's value
- If applicable, dividends to be paid out to shareholders

Section 6 - Balance Sheet

The balance sheet shows your business' debts and assets for long or short term.

The projected balance sheet is a result of the assumptions and other numbers included in the income statement. It should therefore be developed when you are satisfied with the results of your income statement.

If you are operating a new business you can use industry ratios and adjust them according to investments in equipment (assets) and its effect on long-term debt liabilities.

If your business has been in operations for a few years, you can use historical ratios applied to the new projected sales figures which usually follow a similar pattern. Remember that new investments must also be taken into account.

You can also increase current assets and current (short term) liabilities by the percentage of sales growth you forecasted in your projected income statement since they also usually follow a similar pattern.

In current liabilities, you can estimate the expected annual repayment of long term debt you intend to make.

Special projects and equipment or technology expenditures should be incorporated into long term assets (net fixed assets) to reflect the long term nature of their contribution to the company's ongoing operations. Be sure to subtract the estimated accumulated amortization.

For long term liabilities, take the last year's balance sheet number plus the borrowing you intend to do minus repayments in the current year.

Your total assets vs. total liabilities must be the same on the balance sheet; thus the name "Balance Sheet".

Example Balance Sheet - 2011

ASSETS   LIABILITES_____

Cash	Bank loan
Accounts Receivable	Accounts payable
Inventory	Accruals
Prepaid Expenses	Current Portion of LTD
Other _____	Other _____
Current Assets	*Current Liabilities*
Land	Term Debt
Building	Shareholders Advances
Furniture	Other _____
Equipment	*Long-Term Liabilities*
Other _____	
Net Fixed Assets	Common Shares
	Preferred Shares
Research and Development	Retained Earnings
Other Asset _____	Contributed Surplus
Other Assets	**TOTAL SHAREHOLDER EQUITY**
= _____	= _____

TOTAL ASSETS _____   **LIABILITY + SHAREHOLDER EQUITY**

_ _____

LTD stands for Long Term Debt

Section 7 - Cash Flow

A positive or a negative cash flow will determine how your business will use its loans.

A positive cash flow means that your business can meet its short term obligations. A negative cash flow means that you will need to use short-term financing from a line of credit, working capital, personal investment etc.

A cash flow budget will allow you to foresee how much money you will need and when you will need it. This budget has to be completed on a monthly basis for the next two years.

Example Projected Cash Flow

2012	1ˢᵗ Q	Jan	Feb	Mar
Collection of sales				
Loans / Investments				
Sale of assets				
Other_____				
Total Source				

Purchase payment
Direct labor wages
Repairs & Maintenance
Utilities & Taxes
Sales Expenses
Administrative Expenses
Interest
Repayment of debt
Other_____
    Total Expenses
        Surplus / Deficit

Opening cash position
    CASH / LOAN REQUIRED $_____

It is important to measure the impact of your scenarios set earlier in the income statement on this budget. You may need to move some activities to other months to take into account seasonality of sales, necessary investments or cash disbursements.

All **sources of funds** must be listed in the month they are expected to be received such as:

- Collection of sales (should follow the seasonality of sales)
- Interest and revenue on loans and investments
- Sale of assets (usually a lump sum)
- Others (paybacks/rebates from suppliers, interests on credit terms to clients, recuperation of bad debts, etc.) *This amount should be small compared to sales.*

All **expenses** must be listed in the month they are expected to be disbursed and include:

- Purchase payments (raw materials, finished goods, equipment and tools, general operating expenses)
- Salaries when paid (consider number of pays in the month)
- Repayment of debt (capital and interest)
- Other expenses listed under expenses

Be sure to take into account any seasonal changes like:

- An increase in the number of employees during Christmas for example.
- The timetable for purchasing raw materials could change because of growing season.

- Shipping of parts (for equipment) during the summer months is less expensive than in winter.

Also remember that some sales made in month X might not be paid until month Y, depending on the credit terms you negotiate. Annual payments such as taxes can be divided into twelve equal payments.

A surplus allows your business to invest, purchase equipment, pay back loans or reward shareholders but a deficit will require the use of a short-term loan or a personal investment.

Section 8 - Financial Requirements

In this section you will list what financing you will need and why. Some examples could be for purchasing assets such: as land or a building, equipment, or furniture. It can be for research and development or for short-term working capital.

For Assets – List all long term assets (land, equipment, etc.) you intend to buy in the coming two years to achieve your sales target. You should also include shorter-term assets such as investments by shareholders, inflow of working capital, etc. Detail any financing you have already secured, including the name of the financial institution, the purpose of the loan and the type of loan (term loan, venture capital, etc.). You should also give the amount still left to be repaid, the maturity date, the interest rate, and your repayment schedule.

Example Financial Requirements 2012 / 2013

Land
Building
Equipment & Machinery
Furniture & Fixtures
Research & Development_____
Total Assets

Working Capital_____
Total Others

Existing Loan 1

1. Creditor:
2. Purpose of loan:
3. Type of loan:

- Operating loan
- Term loan
- Subordinate debt
- Lease
- Mortgage
- Letter of credit
- Line of credit
- Revolving credit
- Other

4. Collateral:
5. Outstanding debt amount:
6. Maturity date:
7. Interest rate:
8. Repayment schedule:

- Weekly
- Monthly
- Quarterly
- Semi-annually
- Other

9. Repayment method:

- Blended + interest
- Blended
- Interest only
- Other

Section 9 - Performance Indicators

Your banker will compare your numbers and ratios to industry averages to get a clear picture of your financial plan.

*You better make sure you check the numbers and ratios before he/she does.

Example Performance Indicators

	Historical	
	Nov 09	Nov 10
Current Ratio		
Age of Accounts Receivable		
Inventory Turnover Rate		
Interest Coverage		
Total Debt to Equity (%)		
Return on Investment (%)		
Return on Assets (%)		

Asset Turnover Rate
Cash Flow Coverage

Section 10 - Personal Status

Give the personal status of your company's main principals and their families. This information allows your banker to understand you better and it also provides information on the resources you can make available to your business.

Yes, you read that right. Your banker will want you to put your own money into the business before he is willing to put his in. He knows that if you are fully committed to your business you will not just walk away when the times get tough; and they will get tough.

For first time entrepreneurs this section provides information on your background and your abilities to manage your new business.

Note: Since a new company does not have any credit or a track record of repayment, you must be prepared to become personally responsible for any loans to your business.

Your income – Indicate all the amounts and sources of income and identify it as regular or temporary.

Your assets – Show the balance in cash of your bank account/s, in RRSPs, the purchase value of life insurance policies, the value of automobiles and other effects such as furniture, and the book value of your investments.

Liabilities – Show the outstanding balances for all loans.

Example of required Personal Status information

DIRECTOR / OWNER N° 1
1. Last, First Name:
2. Address:
3. Phone:
4. D.O.B.
5. Social:
6. Email:
7. Present employer:
8. Employer's phone:
9. How long at current job:
10. Salary:
11. Last employer if less than 3 years:

FAMILY
1. Your status: (married, single, etc)
2. N° of dependents:
3. *If applicable* Spouse's Last, First name:
4. D.O.B:
5. Social
6. Occupation:
7. Name of employer:
8. Employer's phone:

FINACIAL STATUS

SOURCE OF INCOME | ANNUAL AMOUNT

_____|_____

_____|_____

_____|_____

ASSETS
Cash
RRSPs
Life insurance
Real estate
Automobiles
Stocks, bonds, etc
Household effects

LIBILITES
Bank loans
Credit cards
Mortgages, etc
_____
Total Liabilities

Total Assets   **Total Net Worth** _____

One last thing I feel is worth mentioning. Check your work; you only get one chance to make a first impression.

When I am done a financial plan I like to ask my friend Ravi for his opinion.

R- Re-Read
A- Re-Analyze
V- Re-Verify
I- Invite an accountant to read it over before you present it. Even if it cost you $100 for his opinion it is worth it.

Note: This is a condensed version of your Business Plan and is a separate document.

Executive Summary

ABC WIDGET INC.

123 Street, Suite 456, Big City, State/Province
Zip/Postal Code (800)-555-1212

Prepared: January 1st 2012
by: Your Name and Position

CHAPTER 10

EXECUTIVE SUMMARY

The executive summary is where your banker, lawyer, accountant or other stakeholders will get their first and often final idea of your project. This is also the document that you will present to potential partners. In a few pages, the reader has to get a clear understanding of what your business does, what it wants to achieve and how you will achieve it. This is the crucial element of your business plan.

For your convenience, Appendix D has an example of a blank executive summary which is also downloadable from our website in greater detail. www.kaizerconsulting.com

Example of Introductory Statement:

Kaizer Consulting provides guidance; by way of direct tools, methodology, and knowledge, to anyone wanting to achieve a business related goal.

Business Related Goals:

The goal for any business is almost always to make income directly or indirectly from the completion of one or more major goals and/or a combination of several smaller goals. This includes non-profit organizations where the income generated is used for the benefit of others.

For Startups

The goals can be:

- Deciding how or what products and services to sell.
- What type of business registration is best?
- Best industry design for a website.
- How to hire qualified employees?
- Where to source supplies?
- How to obtain capital needed?
- Etc...

For Established Companies

There is a continual goal in the form of scheduled evaluations and analysis of the current business activities including but not limited to:

- The effectiveness of the marketing plan.

- Competencies of the employees, staff, suppliers, and others.
- Efficiencies of current systems and processes. Ex: Is owning the manufacturing plant still more cost effective than outsourcing the production?

Kaizer Consulting functions as a bridge for information and knowledge and as an external consult we can provide these bridging services more economically than client firms themselves because we have a greater diversity of experience outside the client company.

<u>Why Our Services are in Demand:</u>

Certain evaluations should only be done by external consultants who do not have any bias or concerns for the employees who may need to be let go or replaced; including the possible redundancies of an internal auditor's own position within the company.

For government agencies and/or established companies day to day operation is the closing of one project and starting another usually at the same time; all while continually monitoring and controlling other projects. The cost to these companies of training internal employees to perform each service is a major problem. Only external consultants can quickly replace one knowledge based expert with another.

Since project management is the foundation of Kaizer Consulting, each customer can be sure of a completely professional and well thought out plan.

Objectives of the Plan and Description of the Project

Describe the project (ex: investment, expansion, acquisition, etc.) you want to sell to potential partners, bankers or other stakeholders.

- Why this plan?
- What are your goals in preparing this document?

The reason for creating this business plan was because it is a mandatory step in preparing a solid business foundation. It is the most valuable "tool" Kaizer Consulting will ever have because it is a detailed description of our business activities including what we sell and how we sell it.

The reason for putting this plan in this portable readable format was to sell as a published piece at book stores and online as a guide to be followed for people wanting to start a business. It is as much a guide to the stakeholders of Kaizer Consulting as it is a product to generate income for the company.

What we accomplished during the process of writing this business plan was an in-depth analysis of each activity and event to find and repair any weaknesses that may impact future profitability by answering many questions.

Note: Some of these questions may not apply to your business.

Sales and Marketing Accomplishments

- We identified who our customers will be.
    1. The list can be found in the main body of our plan located on Page _____ (give page number).
- We have identified a particular age group (if you were selling age specific products)
    2. The age group _____ accounts for _____ % of our line _____...
- We have identified how we plan to attract customers.
    3. This is outlined on page _____ of our main plan.
- We have determined the best marketing strategy for our individual products and services.
    4. As detailed on page _____...
- We have calculated what the marketing budget will be.
    5. This amount is found on page _____...
- Etc…

Finance Accomplishments

- We have determined the payment terms for your customers.

6. Do the same for each accomplishment. You do not need to list the results of every accomplishment but identify where those results can be found.

- We now know how we will collect accounts receivables.
- We know if we need long term debt?
- We can say what financial reports need to be generated.
- And know how often.
- We have determined what the best filing system will be for our business.
- Etc…

Management Accomplishments

- We know how many employees will be needed.
- We know how many people will be in a management position.
- We have figured out how we will we get the required results from our people.
- We have shown how we have been successful in this kind of business before.
- Proper preparation of documented standards and procedures for our people are done
- Development of training manuals are done

Vision Accomplishments

- We know what our corporate vision is and how to achieve our goals.

Business History and Nature of Operation
Again just take what you have already written and put it into a very condensed form.

Products and Services

Provide a condensed version of your Sales and Marketing plan with a small introduction. Remember that the reader has not seen the rest of your plan.

Example:
Kaizer Consulting operates under the parameters of Project Management so our products and services are completely synergetic. Providing one main service usually includes several other services. The services are listed below with a description.

1.   **Business Registration** involves either choosing a name and doing a name search and receiving a reservation number which is needed for the incorporation process. I prefer registering a federal numbered company since it is easy and there is no wait time for name approval. Then you can register a trade name later after you find an acceptable website name, which leads to the next service:

2.   **Website Development** is mandatory because these days if your business doesn't have an online presence it doesn't exist. But just having a URL does not mean you will attract potential customers. A website is part of the overall operation

of your business model and is the most major part of your marketing. Website development involves finding and registering a URL (web name), figuring out the best hosting plan; that alone involves determining how much data will be utilized, how many email address are needed, what type of databases are needed, what type of systems integration will be designed, setting up a proper security protocol, designing forms, determining the site layout by industry, showing the client how to use the options, setting up proper internet marketing, and the list can be endless.

3. **Marketing** is very necessary but often overlooked when funds are tight. But before deciding to spend what funds you have on any marketing you must first determine what type of advertizing is best for your industry, what your financial limitations are, and who your particular target audience is.

4. Our **Business Plan Services** is the most important service to utilize. If you already have a business plan you know that routine maintenance is necessary to keep your company operating at optimum levels. Your business plan is the most valuable tool you can have. A business plan is a detailed description of your business, it is a map of your businesses' future; a poorly done business plan is a map to a poor future, but is still better than not having one at all. According to Statistics Canada 80% of all businesses fail here in Canada and in the rest of the world. That means that for every 10

people you know who own their own business, 8 will fail. The reason is because they are wandering in the wilderness without a map or compass to guide them. They think that if they just keep going they will eventually find civilization. Well I can guarantee that they won't. Not having a business plan is fine if you don't plan on ever really growing, ever getting a business loan or getting investors. It is also fine if you never want to sell your business or get the big customers. And it is also fine if you always want to be the one doing all the hard work. But then why are you in business to start with if you don't want anything?

Part of the business plan writing service includes "Business Analysis" and is used to help us get a preliminary understanding of a business' current strengths and weaknesses, calculate impact on profitability and determine a course of action. Some of these questions may seem basic and rudimentary but all serve a specific purpose. A few examples are:

Note: This section will look like it has been repeated. When you input your company's products and services that will change.

Business History:

- What is your industry?
- How long has your business been operating?
- Why did you start the business?
- What has your experience been so far?

- Do you have a business plan?
- Do you have documented goals?
- Have you reached any of your goals?
- Do you keep track of time spent in your business activities?
- Do you keep track of business appointments in a scheduler?
- Have you made changes to try to improve the business?
- Have you consulted with external experienced business advisors?

Sales and marketing

- Who are your customers?
- What age group do you target?
- How to you attract customers?
- Do you get referral business?
- What marketing have you tried?
- Do you know how to analyze the outcomes of your chosen marketing?
- Do you have a marketing budget?

Finance

- Are you profitable?
- What are your payment terms with customers?
- Do you make an effort to collect accounts receivables?
- Are you paying your bills on time?
- Do you have long term debt?
- What financial reports do you generate?

- How often?
- Do you keep copies of receipts in a filing system?

Management

- How many employees do you have?
- How many people are in a management position?
- Are you getting the results you want from your people?
- Have you been successful in this kind of business before?
- Do you have documented standards and procedures for your people?
- Do you have training manuals?

Vision

- What is your vision for your company?
- What are some key challenges for your business?
- Etc...

5.   **Security Services** is both a stand alone service and part of many other services such as: web design, database management, and risk assessment. Kaizer Consulting has licensed personnel with the ability to intellectually and physically blend in to any environment and are experienced at designing a proper Technical Security Program. For more see Products and

Services section in the business plan main document.

6. **Risk Assessment** ensures that an organization identifies and understands the risks to which it is exposed. Risk management also creates and implements an effective plan to prevent or reduce the impact of a particular risk event. While it is not literally possible to see the unforeseen, a good risk management plan includes strategies and techniques to recognize and confront all possible threats and determine the consequences of occurrence. This is done by asking questions which lead to more questions. What can go wrong? What are the implications? What will we do if it happens? How do we prevent it from happening? How do we lessen its effects? What is the difference in cost to prevent it from happening versus the cost after it happens? Like traffic lights telling you when to stop and go, a good risk management plan let you know when it is safe to proceed in business.

7. **Human Resource Services** involves implementing best practices to ensure the supply of skilled and qualified individuals and enhance the capabilities of the current workforce. Aligning with the organizations' ongoing and future business plans and requirements to maximize return on investment and secure future survival and success. Kaizer Consulting can provide: a) Full testing capabilities to ensure the potential hire possesses all the required knowledge for the position. b) Complete screening of applicants for security

clearances. c) Psychological and Psychometric testing. d) Candidate interviews, etc.

Project financing

Summarize the financial requirements section from the separate excel spreadsheet. This is an outline of your financial plan; the project (asset acquisition, business development, etc.) and how you intend to finance it (own funds, investments, loans, equity, etc.). Explain the type of financing your business will eventually ask from its banker/s.

Management and advisors

Describe who you are and who the people who support you are. Investors, bankers, even stakeholders, want to know who does (or is going to) manage this company. This section gives credibility to your plan. Do not restrict yourself to shareholders; consider advisors as well.

1. Your name
Your title/s
Your credentials and every reason why you are capable of running this business

2. Your partners name
His/Her title/s
Their credentials and every reason why they are qualified to be running the business

3. The name of an experienced or expert advisor or mentor
Include their credentials and experience.

4. The name of all persons that will aid you in making this business a success.

Risk Assessment and Contingency Plan

Although the name "Risk Assessment and Contingency Planning" seems like a completely different and separate procedure from business planning it is not. In fact all the parameters of the risk assessment and contingency plan are formed as a result of completing other steps in the business plan.

Different organizations are subject to different risks, but what every organization has in common is the way in which they determine what is at risk. The answers may be different but the questions are always the same:

- What can go wrong?
- What are the chances it will go wrong?
- How will it affect us if it does?
- How can we prevent it from happening?
- What can we do to lessen its affects?
- How do we handle when it does?

For a business you need to know:

- What are the chances, and under what conditions, this business would not succeed as expected? Ex: sales do not materialize, profits do not come, expenses are higher than planned, etc.
- What are you going to do to ensure the survival of the business? Ex: ease with which assets can be disposed of, guaranteed business/sales, strengths/expertise in sectors, etc.

The easiest way to do this is to make a chart with five columns with the headings; Risk, probability of Occurrence, the affect of occurrence on Cost, and affect on Schedule. Use the ratings - High = 3, Med = 2, and Low = 1
The amount of rows will be determined by the amount of risks that could affect your business.
The more risks you think of the better because it will help you to thoroughly grasp your business and will show your banker or anyone else viewing the document you have a real understanding of all of the risks that could affect your business.

It is very hard for the first timer to "guess" all of the risks that could affect your business. A lot of risks are unforeseen and trying to foresee the unforeseen is impossible.

Based on the type of business you have chosen, list all of the factors (risks) that could affect your business. As mentioned different organizations will have different risks. A sample chart shows what type of risks affect Kaizer Consulting.

You may wonder why air conditioning is the first risk listed. Air conditioning is a major risk factor to businesses that operate in high heat and high humidity locations. It has an effect on not only the health and safety of the employees but also their performance and output. This is also true for businesses that do not have employees since heat and humidity affects equipment and electronics in the same way as humans.

Contingency or preventative measures already taken or planned are below each item.

Risk	O	C	S	C + S
Air Conditioning Failure	1	1	1	2
No cause for alarm				
Blackmail	1	1	1	2
No cause for alarm				
Hacking/Cyber attack	1	2	2	4
High security in place lower possibility of occurrence. Data backups enable fast access and restoration of business. Cost and schedule would only be affected if hack damaged hardware and needed to be replaced.				
Sabotage/Vandalism Break in	1	2	1	3
High security on all systems and facility lowers available time for sabotage or vandalism. Proximity of facility to government buildings lowers police response times.				
Chemical spill/	1	1	1	2

HazMat				
No chemicals are on location				
Cold/Frost/Snow/ Storms	**3**	1	2	3
High probability of occurrence. Schedule will only be affected slightly if communication is disrupted.				
Communications loss	**3**	1	2	3
High probability of occurrence. Schedule is only affected if hard lines and wireless communication is affected simultaneously.				
Data Disruption	**3**	1	2	3
High probability of occurrence. Related to communication loss to main server and back ups.				
Data Loss	1	**3**	**3**	**6**
Low probability of occurrence. Systems automatically save and back up data even if not manually saved. However if system recovery programs can not restore data from any source everything will have to be redone from scratch.				
Fire	**2**	**3**	**2**	**5**
Fire is always a possibility. If fire destroys all hardware it will have to be replaced. Schedule will be affected only as long as it takes to set up new hardware in back up location.				
Earthquake	2	2	2	4
The location is near a fault line so an earthquake is possible. However past earthquakes have proven nearly damage free.				
Flooding/Water damage	1	1	1	2
Water damage from flooding would only occur in spring. However none of the equipment would be				

			affected by a flood.	
Power Loss/Outage	**3**	1	1	2
Occasional temporary power outages have occurred in this area during winter months. However all systems are on back up power sources preventing any disruption.				
Terror Attack	1	**3**	**3**	**6**
Very low probability of occurrence. Even if location is not directly affected, the local and possibly international business economy could grind to a halt.				
Terror Threat	2	1	2	3
Threats happen all the time but do not usually affect business.				
Nuclear Mishap	1	1	1	2
Low probability of occurrence. There are no nuclear reactors close to the location.				
Unemployment	2	1	2	3
Unemployment is on the rise in Canada. Schedule is only affected if there is also a freeze on spending.				
Recession	**3**	1	2	3
A recession is eminent in Canada. Schedule will be affected if there is a freeze on spending.				
Credit Crunch	2	1	2	3
Credit is given more freely in a recession to promote hiring.				
Regulation and Compliance	2	1	2	3
Won't affect company.				
Radical Greening	1	1	1	2
Won't affect Company				
Cost Cutting	2	1	**3**	4

	Will affect schedule.			
Talent Risk	1	1	1	2
	Large pool of Candidates to choose from.			
Business Model Redundancies	1	1	1	2
	Continual innovation prevents this.			
Reputation Risk	1	1	1	2
	Proven methods.			
Demand Risk	2	1	**3**	4
	Only affected with cost cutting.			

Financial Institution

Even if you are only dealing with your own bank you still need to include your banking details to enable the pairing of your business plan to your loan application.

Any outside investor and/or banker will need even more information to validate the claimed information about your business.

These details are:

- The name of the account; which is either your name in the case of a sole proprietorship or your business' name.
- The physical and/or mailing address the account is set up under including telephone numbers.
- The account number.
- The most recent financial statements.

Supporting Documentation

Before presenting your plan to potential investors, you will need to go back through your plan and identify all the areas that need proof of claim. If you can not provide proof you have to either delete it or have a good explanation why you can't support it.

Startups will always believe that they have a good excuse. Startups think that since they are based solely on forecasted projections they are exempt from providing certain supporting documentation. Unfortunately this is where I tell you that in reality, it is completely the opposite.

Startups have a higher risk associated since there is no track record at all. Even a bad track record is better than no track record. Every company goes through a loss (money burning) phase in the beginning and banks know it.

You have heard these quotes said many times: "Banks only want to give you money when you don't need it". Or: "Where were they when I needed them the most?"

A good analogy would be buying a new car. Everyone knows that a new car depreciates the most in the first year. Eventually if you hold on to it long enough and keep it in perfect condition it has the potential to appreciate. This is exactly what happens to a business except much faster.

The bottom line; You are applying for funding because you need to spend money upfront to acquire certain items that you feel will enable you and your company to perform the services and/or supply the products offered by your company.

Right now I am going to take you back to the beginning of this book. Do you remember when I told you I have walked in many different shoes? Many pairs where worn when I was looking for funding and other pairs where worn while in a position to give funding. So I know what both sides of the equation want to see in a funding request and can tell you that the funder is still not satisfied.

With that said we continue from where we left off; you needing to spend money to acquire the items that will enable you to operate your business…

So let's pretend it is the near future and you were already granted the funds and are in possession of the tools needed to perform the services and/or supply the products offered by your company.

Now what?

Now the investor wants to know how you are going to pay back the loan. The investor knows that the equipment has already lost value and is losing value every minute. You are or have already been spending more of the loaned money on advertizing and other operating expenses. You are burning through the living expenses to feed yourself and your family.

At this point the investor is not at risk of losing his money, he has already lost it. Because it is no longer in his position, nor is it in yours. It has been spent on items that he can not use or sell. For a very small potential of return he is completely at your mercy.

Now that you have seen the not so distant future from the eyes of the investor, let us go back to the present.

If your plan does not detail how you will pay back the loan and include all the supporting documentation you will not get a loan. The supporting documentation can never include too much info but will at very least be:

- Signed contracts from customers
- Resumes of your partners
- Market studies
- Magazine articles that can help you better sell your business plan
- Etc.

Doesn't look like much now does it? Putting yourself in the investors or bankers shoes is the only way for you to understand why a solid business plan is so important.

Good luck!

MANAGING ORGANIZED CHAOS

APPENDIX

A - Financial Glossary
B - Business Questions
C - Business Plan Contents - Checklist
D - Example Executive Summary

Appendix A

FINANCIAL GLOSSARY

A

ACCOUNTS PAYABLE
Amounts owed by a business to its suppliers, usually as a result of credit purchases for inventory or services, other expenses (i.e. utilities), or taxes.

ACCOUNTS RECEIVABLE
Amounts owed to you by your customers (under A/R Trade) or other entities (under Other).

ACCRUALS
Amounts due to employees but not yet disbursed, sales tax collected but not yet sent on, etc.

ADMINISTRATIVE EXPENSES
Operating costs incurred in the normal course of running a business, such as telephone, management and office salaries, professional fees, property taxes, etc.

AGE OF ACCOUNTS RECEIVABLE
Financial ratio defined as 365 days divided by the accounts receivable turnover. To determine the latter, divide net credit sales by average accounts receivable.

Compute average accounts receivable by adding opening and ending accounts receivable, divide the result by 2

This ratio shows how fast a business is collecting from its customers. The higher the number, the longer it takes the business to receive payment, translating into a possible lack of working capital.

ASSET
Anything owned by a person or a business that has commercial or exchange value. Assets may be tangible or intangible and may include accounts and notes receivable, cash, inventory, equipment, real estate, goodwill, etc.

ASSET TURNOVER
Financial ratio defined as Sales divided by Total assets. It measures the business' use of assets to generate income, more specifically the level of capital investment relative to its sales volume. The higher the turnover, the more efficiently the business is managing its assets.

B

BALANCE SHEET
Financial statement listing all assets, liabilities and equity of a business at a certain point in time. It provides a quick "snapshot" of a business.

BOOK VALUE
Value of an asset as shown on the balance sheet. The book value takes into account depreciation and is often different from its market value.

BREAK-EVEN POINT

The point in time at which a new business' revenues (dollar volume of sales) equals its fixed and variable expenses.

BUDGET
An estimate of future income and expenses over an accounting period (quarterly, yearly, etc.) used as a financial control for business.

BUSINESS FINANCING PLAN
An outline of the business goals, the purposes of its loans, and the benefits to the business resulting from the loans. It can also include summaries of historical, market and other data.

C

CAPITAL
The owner's equity in the business. It can take the form of the proprietor's or partners' capital, or, if incorporated, that of common stock, preferred shares and retained earnings.

CASH FLOW BUDGET
A spreadsheet of monthly inflows (e.g., earnings) and outflows (e.g., expenses) of cash in the business during an accounting period, usually 1 year. It helps a business plan its financial requirements.

CLOSING INVENTORY
Value of the total inventory or the number of units that a business has on hand at the end of the accounting period.

COGS
Abbreviated form of Cost of Goods Sold, also called Cost of Sales

CONTRIBUTED SURPLUS

Any capital contributed to a business other than through the issue of shares. It includes share redemption, donation from a shareholder, certain dividend transactions.

CORPORATION
Legal entity incorporated under federal or provincial legislation. This entity is distinct from parties or individuals that own it. Shareholders are not liable for debts or obligations of the corporation.

COST OF SALES / COST OF GOODS SOLD
Abbreviated as COGS, also called cost of sales. Direct cost of producing or providing the business' goods or services. It includes direct labor costs and production overhead plus opening inventory plus purchases less closing inventory.

CURRENT ASSETS
Cash and other assets that, in the normal course of operations, may be converted into cash, or consumed into the production of income within one year from the date of the Balance Sheet. They include cash, accounts receivable, allowance for doubtful accounts, inventory and prepaid expenses.

CURRENT INCOME TAX
Taxes on the income earned by your company that is payable within the next twelve months.

CURRENT LIABILITIES
Outstanding debts of the business that are payable within one year of the date of the Balance Sheet. They include a credit line, accounts payable, accruals (ex. sales tax collected), income tax and current portion of the long term debt.

CURRENT PORTION OF LONG-TERM DEBT
How much you will pay back on your loan (principal, not including interest) this fiscal year

CURRENT RATIO
Financial ratio defined as Current assets divided by Current liabilities that measure the business' ability to meet its current obligations on time and to have funds available for its current operations.

D

DEPRECIATION
The decline of the value of equipment or other assets over time. Your accountant can help you choose the right method for the type of asset.

DEFFERED TAXES
Taxes that will not be paid until a later date. If a company uses a separate accounting method when calculating taxes, any difference between the two methods will be indicated here.

DISBURSEMENTS
Funds paid out of a business in settlement of obligations.

DIVIDENDS
Company earnings that are paid to stockholders

DRAWINGS
Withdrawals of assets (usually cash) from a business by a sole proprietor or a partner.

E

EQUIPMENT
All machinery and equipment used by the business to earn revenue. It has a limited lifespan and thus is subject to depreciation.

F

FINANCIAL STATEMENTS
Formal reports, prepared from accounting records, describing the financial position and performance of the business. They comprise the Balance Sheet, the Income Statement, the Statement of Changes in Financial Position. See also these definitions.

FIXED ASSETS
Also called capital assets. Property or equipment, not intended to be sold, owned by a business for use in its operations and expected to have a useful life of several fiscal periods. Included in this are land, buildings, vehicles, furniture and equipment.

FIXED COSTS
Amounts that do not vary with changes in the volume of sales or production (i.e. rent, depreciation, interest payments).

FORECAST
Estimate or prediction of future sales, expenditures, profits, etc.

FREIGHT & OTHER DUTY
Under Cost of Goods Sold, these represent the amounts paid to transport goods from your suppliers

G

GROSS PROFIT
Net Sales less Cost of Goods Sold. It represents the profit made by the business before deducting selling, administrative and financial expenses. It helps to evaluate sales performance, buying policies, mark-ups, and inventory controls.

I

INCOME STATEMENT
Financial statement showing revenues, expenses and net income of a business over an accounting period.

INCORPORATION
Legal process of bringing a company into existence by filing appropriate documentation with federal or provincial legislation.

INTANGIBLE ASSETS
Assets that cannot be touched, weighed or measured. They cannot be used for payments of debts and include goodwill (probability that a regular customer will remain so), patent, trademark, incorporations costs. They may produce income and can be sold, that is why they are listed under assets.

INTEREST COVERAGE RATIO
Financial ratio defined as Income before interest and taxes divided by Interest expense. It reflects the number of times business income cover interest expenses and represents a safety margin for the business.

INVENTORY
Dollar value (cost or market, whichever is lower) of all stock of physical items that a business uses in its production process or has for sale.

INVENTORY TURNOVER
Financial ratio defined as Cost of goods sold divided by Average inventory. Compute average inventory by adding opening and ending inventory, divide the result by 2. It measures the number of times inventory has been sold in a given year. If it is low, it means that products are not selling well.

L

LABOR EXPENSES
Total direct cost to the business for its employees during an accounting period. Includes actual wages paid and cost of all fringe benefits, unless listed separately.

LEASE
Legal contract covering the use of property drawn up between an owner (lesser) and a tenant (lessee) for a stated amount of money (rent) and for a specified length of time.

LEASEHOLD IMPROVEMENTS
Renovations and other improvements done to the leased property at the expense of the lessee.

LIABILTIES
Amounts owed by the business to its creditors, not necessarily to be paid immediately. An obligation to remit money or services at a future date, ex accounts payable, loans.

LINE OF CREDIT
Agreement between a lender and a borrower under which the latter can borrow continuously up to a fixed maximum amount.

LONG-TERM LIABILITIES
Outstanding term loans less the current portion (see definition of Current Liabilities) that are not due within the next 12 months.

M

MARKET

A group of consumers that can be described in a specific way (e.g., men aged 25 to 35 with an annual income of over $40,000 and living in the target area.)

MATERIAL PURCHASES
Under your Cost Of Sales, all goods that you buy that are directly related to producing your goods or services.

MARKET SEGMENT
Part of a *market* (e.g., men aged 25 to 35 with an annual income of over $40,000 who live in the target area and are interested in the arts)

N

NAIS CODE
North American Industry Classification System -- a standardized system of 6-digit codes to identify industries in Canada, the U.S., and Mexico. It replaces the old 4-digit SIC.

NET PROFIT
Excess of all revenues over all expenses during the same accounting period.

NET PROFIT MARGIN
Net profit divided by sales; expressed as a percentage

NICHE
Part of a *market segment* (e.g., men aged 25 to 35 with an annual income of over $40,000 who live in the Toronto area and are interested specifically in performance arts)

NON-OPERATING ITEMS
Income or expenses that are not part of your company's day to day operations, such as interest earned on investments.

O

OPENING INVENTORY
Value of total inventory or number of units a business has on hand at the opening of the accounting period.

OPERATING FORECAST
Anticipated earnings of a business determined by estimating sales and subtracting expected expenses.

OPERATING PROFIT / OPERATING INCOME
Excess of revenue of a business over its expenses, excluding income derived from sources other than its regular activities, i.e. extraordinary income and expenses, income taxes, dividends, bonuses, withdrawals by owners.

OVERHEAD
Costs not directly attributable to the production of a good, ex. salary of factory manager, property taxes.

P

PARTNERSHIP
Form of business ownership in which two or more individuals (or companies) provide the equity capital for a business enterprise. Partners share in the profits as well as the losses of the business.

PREPAID EXPENSES
Expenses paid in advance during an accounting period (ex. a two-year insurance premium), part of which will be "used up" in the upcoming accounting period. The unused portion of the expense is considered a current asset and recorded as such on the Balance Sheet.

PROFESSIONAL FEES

Fees paid for professional services (for example, accountants, lawyers, or consultants).

PROFIT
Total revenue less total expenses for an accounting period calculated in accordance with generally accepted accounting principles.

PUBLIC SERVICES
Costs for services typically provided by public corporations, such as electricity, water, and gas.

R

RATIO ANALYSIS
Analysis that compares financial ratios of a business from one year to another to determine the change in performance over time; it also compares financial ratios of a business to that of other similar businesses or to that of its industry to determine its performance in relation to others.

REPAIRS & MAINTENANCE
Costs related to the upkeep of your equipment. You can estimate this from historical data, use a percentage of equipment cost, or use life cycle data or outsourced maintenance contract costs

RETAINED EARNINGS
Profits not spent or distributed among owners of a business but reinvested in it.

RETURN ON ASSETS
Financial ratio defined as Net income plus Interest expense (net of tax) divided by Total assets. It indicates how efficiently the business has used its available resources to generate income

RETURN ON INVESTMENT

Financial ratio defined as Net income after taxes divided by Average shareholders' equity. Compute the latter by adding opening and ending balances, divide the result by 2. It measures the profitability of the business for its shareholders.

REVENUE
Gross proceeds received by a business from the sale of goods or services during an accounting period. It also includes gains from the sale or exchange of assets, interest and dividends earned on investments and other increases in owner's equity.

S

SALARIES
Employees' salaries are generally listed separately from management's. It is also common practice to separate salaries that are related to production (put under Cost of Goods Sold), sales (put under Sales Expenses) and administration (put under Expenses).

SALES
Total value of goods sold or revenue from services rendered. Returns and discounts must be shown as a reduction from total sales.

SALES EXPENSES
Operating costs directly related to the selling of a product or service (selling salaries, commission, advertising, etc).

SERVICES & UTILITIES
Costs for services typically provided by public corporations, such as electricity, water, and gas.

SHAREHOLDERS EQUITY
Net assets (i.e., minus liabilities) that belong to owners of the business.

SHIPPING & DELIVERY
Under Expenses, costs related to shipping goods from your suppliers and to your clients.

SIC
Standard Industrial Classification (SIC) - a system of 4-digit codes for identifying various industries, devised in the U.S. in the 1930s. This has been replaced by the NAICS.

SOLE PROPRIETORSHIP
Form of business owned and operated by one individual who is responsible for the debts and obligations of the business.

STATEMENT OF CHANGES IN FINANCIAL POSITION
Financial statement showing the fluctuation of capital of a business over an accounting period.

T

TERM LOAN
Loan having a fixed term of repayment greater the one year, and a monthly or seasonal principal reduction schedule.

TOTAL DEBT-TO-EQUITY RATIO
Financial ratio defined as Total liabilities divided by Shareholders' equity. It measures the solvency of the business: if this ratio is high, the business is at higher risk of not meeting its obligations should a drop in sales occur.

V

VARIABLE COSTS

Expenses that vary directly with changes in the volume of sales or production, e.g. raw material costs and sales commissions.

W

WORKING CAPITAL
Financial ratio defined as Current assets minus Current liabilities. It represents the amount of cash a business has to develop itself as opposed to the capital it has invested in fixed assets. A high ratio means the business can convert some assets into cash or obtain cash readily to meet its current obligations and represents a safety cushion for creditors.

Appendix B

BUSINESS QUESTIONS

Questions are the most major part of any business. Questions in general are fundamental to investigating and researching everything imaginable.

To figure out where we want to go and find out how to get there we must first determine where we (or others) have been. For a business owner the question may be; how was X business able to achieve their success, and how will I achieve mine.

The following is some of the many topics pertaining to past clients and other business owners I have had the pleasure of working with. Over time I have incorporated the topics into various questionnaires that I present to new clients so we can both get an idea of how I can help. These questions are certainly not inclusive since questions lead to more and even more questions during the evolution of your business.

The point of this exercise (questionnaires) is to teach you how each part of your business fits into the synergy of the whole. Please feel free to add to or modify the questions to suit your needs.

Questionnaire Example

Please answer each question with a YES or NO then above the number of questions in that section, enter the number of times you answered YES.

I. BUSINESS LIKE MANNER

1. Do you have or will you have a separate bank account for your business?
Y N

2. Do you or will you keep accounting records for the business?
Y N

3. Do you or will you keep copies of receipts in a filling system?
Y N

4. Do you or will you make an effort to collect AR (accounts receivables?
Y N

5. Do you or will you review profit and loss statements regularly?
Y N

___ (times you answered YES)
5 (number of questions in this section)

II. TIME AND EFFORT

1. Do you or will you keep track of time spent in your business activity?
Y N

2. Do you or will you keep track of business appointments in a scheduler or diary?
Y N

3. Do you or will you keep notes of conversations you have with consultants or experts to enhance your business?
Y N

4. Do you or will you keep evidence from business seminars you have attended?
Y N

5. Do you or will you create and keep to-do lists?
Y N

5

III. DEPEND ON INCOME

1. Will you or do you need the income from your business for your lifestyle?
Y N

2. Do you intend to replace your current job with this business? Answer yes if you already have.
Y N

2

IV. LOSSES

If you have losses, do you have documentation that:

1. They are normal for the type of business you are in?
Y N

2. That others in the same type of business have experienced the same kind of losses?
Y N

2

V. EFFORT TO MAKE MONEY

1. Have you made changes to try to improve your business?
Y N

2. Have you investigated ways to make your business more profitable?
Y N

3. You have read books written by experienced professionals to learn how to make money.
Y N
3 was answered for you

3

VI. EXPERIENCED ADVISORS

1. Have you consulted with experienced business owners or other advisors regarding your business?
Y N

2. Have you identified the advisors you need for your business?
Y N

3. Do your advisors have the business experience needed to give you good advice?
Y N

4. Do you even know how to determine whether or not an advisor actually has the business experience (knowledge) needed to give you good advice?
Y N

4

VII. PERSONAL EXPERIENCE

1. Have you been successful in running this kind of business before?
Y N

2. Have you been successful in running a similar business?
Y N

3. Has any of your business partners (people who will be running the day to day operations with you) been successful in running this kind of business before?
Y N

4. Have they been successful in running a similar business?
Y N

5. Have you or any of your partners been successful in running any business before?
Y N

5

VIII. PAST PROFIT

1. Has this business been profitable in previous years?
Y N

2. If so, has the profit been enough to make it sensible to continue?
Y N

2

IX. ASSET APPRECIATION

1. Is the business building assets that will have future appreciation?
Y N

1

Now go back and divide the top number (number of YES answers) by the bottom number (number of questions) to get a percentage shown in decimal form.

Example: $\frac{3}{5} = 0.6$ which is 60%

I. BUSINESS LIKE MANNER	_____%
II. TIME AND EFFORT	_____%
III. DEPEND ON INCOME	_____%
IV. REASONABLE LOSSES	_____%
V. EFFORT TO MAKE MONEY	_____%
VI. EXPERIENCED ADVISORS	_____%
VII. YOUR EXPERIENCE	_____%

VIII. PAST PROFIT   _____%
IX. ASSET APPRECIATION   _____%

The scores above show the areas of your business that need to be worked on? 100% is always the goal.

I have included even more questions that may be of help to evaluate your business. You can create your own questionnaire or you can use them as brain storming tools. You can answer TRUE or FALSE or modify them to generate other answers.

LEADERSHIP

1. I am so busy that I often lose sight of what's important to me.

2. I can't seem to find the right balance between my work and personal life.

3. I don't have a clear idea of what I want from my business.

4. My employees don't seem to care about their work the way I would like them to.

5. My employees don't have a clear picture of what this business is all about.

6. I don't know how to gauge whether my business is on the right tract.

7. I'm so busy fighting fires; I never seem to get anything done.

8. I don't know how to motivate others to do their best.

9. I don't feel like I am a true leader.

10. I don't feel like I'm in control of how I spend my time.

11. I work too many hours.

12. Other concerns I have in the areas of leadership are:

MARKETING

1. My company doesn't do enough marketing.

2. I don't know what type of person is most likely to buy from my company.

3. I don't know what distinguishes us from our competitors.

4. I don't think that my potential customers know what distinguishes us from our competition

5. I don't think that our current customers know what distinguishes us from the competition.

6. I don't think our marketing program is effective.

7. I don't know how to determine whether our marketing is effective.

8. We don't have a clearly defined company image.

9. Our marketing doesn't have a clear, consistent message.

10. I don't know how to, or think that we can't, use a target marketing plan.

11. I don't know how to, or we don't, develop and use marketing plans.

12. Other concerns about marketing:

_____

MONEY

1. I don't feel that I am in control of my company's money.
2. I am not satisfied with our company's financial record keeping.

3. I frequently don't have enough cash to meet current needs.

4. I don't know what my financial goals are.

5. I am not sure where we stand in relation to our financial goals.

6. I don't receive regular financial statements.

7. I receive regular financial statements, but don't feel that I know what to look for.

8. I am not achieving the profit margins I would like.

9. I don't know what profit margins are, or why they are important.

10. I don't know what my business is worth.

11. I don't know how to prepare or use a budget.

12. Other concerns about money:

_____

MANAGEMENT

1. My company is disorganized, work accountabilities and reporting relationships are not clear.

2. My employees rarely know what they should be doing. They need constant supervision.

3. My employees know what to do, but the quality of their work is far below what I would like.

4. I would be in big trouble if certain key person(s) in my business were to leave.

5. I am not able to find and keep good employees on a consistent basis.

6. Staff training is a big problem in my company.

7. Work never gets done the same way twice.

8. Employee problems take up too much of my time.

9. We don't know how to do, or don't take the time for, employee performance evaluations.

10. My managers don't know how to manage.

11. Employees frequently complain about their managers, and/or managers complain about their employees.

12. Other concerns about management:

LEAD GENERATION

1. Not having enough leads is a big problem for me.

2. I don't know if we're doing enough advertising.

3. I don't know how to evaluate the effectiveness of our advertising.

4. We spend too much on advertising and get too little return.

5. I don't know the bet way for my company to generate leads.

6. I don't know where my best leads come from.

7. We don't know how to ask for or get referrals.

8. I don't know what the best methods are for reaching the people I want to reach.

9. We don't have a large enough budget to generate leads effectively.

10. Lead generation is too complicated for a company like mine.
11. We don't know how to implement or evaluate our lead generation activities.

12. Other concerns about lead generation:

_____

LEAD CONVERSION

1. We're not making enough sales.

2. My salespeople are not able to generate predictable results each month.

3. I don't know how to sell our product/service/ as effectively as I would like.

4. I know how to sell our product/service, but nobody else in the company does.

5. I believe that you can't teach someone to be a good salesperson: they are either born with it or they are not.

6. I don't know, or don't care, what our lead conversion rate is.

7. My salespeople all sell our product/service differently.

8. We don't know how to overcome objections.

9. I am not sure what I can do to increase sales from my existing customers.

10. I have no way to measure the effectiveness of our sales effort.

11. I don't know how to manage salespeople; I often don't know what they are doing.

12. Other concerns about lead conversion:

_____

CLIENT FULFILLMENT

1. I don't know whether clients are satisfied or not.

2. I don't think the quality of our product/service is as high as it should be.

3. The quality of our product/service is inconsistent; sometimes it is very good and sometimes it is not.

4. I don't understand why our product/service quality is so inconsistent.

5. I don't know what our client retention rate is.

6. We lose too many clients for no good reason.

7. I often worry that we won't complete the client's job on time.

8. Capacity planning is a problem for me.

9. I don't know how to improve our client fulfillment systems.

10. We don't have any or enough client fulfillment systems; things just seem to get done by individuals who "know" in their heads what to do.

11. We're constantly putting out fires.

12. Other concerns about client fulfillment:

Appendix C

BUSINESS PLAN CONTENTS CHECKLIST

The items contained in this checklist have been determined to be the most frequently included items in a business plan. You should include information on every topic listed and even take the time to add others that you feel your particular plan may benefit from.

By combining the results of the example questionnaire from Appendix B - Business Questions, it is possible to identify additional items to include in your plan.

INTRODUCTORY ELEMENTS

- ☐ Cover and title page
- ☐ Table of contents: You may use the table of contents in the front of this book.

☐ Statement and purpose of the business plan: The information developed here will be duplicated in various sections of the business plan.

☐ Company strategies

☐ Company story: Business overview, background, reason for starting will all be included here.

COMPANY DEVELOPMENT/GROWTH PLAN

☐ Development Goals: Use the SMART goal system discussed in CHAPTER 8

☐ Assumptions

☐ Schedule

☐ Budget and Sources of funds

CORPORATE PLAN

☐ Systems Development Plan

☐ Organizational Strategy

☐ Leadership Plan

☐ Management Plan and Personnel Plan (staffing)

☐ Description of key management systems

☐ Quantification Plan - Reporting vehicles (how you will measure performance)

MARKETING PLAN

- ☐ Marketing Goals
- ☐ Overall description of general market
- ☐ Company image and positioning, external market forces (competition, laws and regulations)
- ☐ Specific Market Segments (target market description (demographics))
- ☐ Positioning and Marketing Strategy
- ☐ Quantification Plan - Reporting vehicles

FINANCIAL PLAN

- ☐ Financial Goals
- ☐ Overall Financial Strategy (pricing plan)
- ☐ Description of key financial systems and reports
- ☐ History of financial performance
- ☐ Pro-forma financial statements
- ☐ Projections
- ☐ Financial Summary

CLIENT FULFULLMENT PLAN

- ☐ Client Fulfillment Goals
- ☐ Products/Services
- ☐ Production Strategy (if applicable)

☐ Service Strategy
☐ Delivery Strategy: Will include all steps from payment to delivery.
☐ Customer Service Strategy
☐ Quantification Plan - Reporting vehicles

LEAD CONVERSION PLAN

☐ Lead Conversion Goals
☐ Lead Conversion - Sales Personnel
☐ Lead Conversion - Sales processes and key systems
☐ Quantification Plan - Reporting vehicle

LEAD GENERATION PLAN

☐ Lead Generation Goals
☐ Lead Generation Channels
☐ Lead Generation - Process and key systems
☐ Quantification Plan - Reporting vehicle

OTHER STRATIGIES AND FACTORS NOT MENTIONED

☐ _____
☐ _____
☐ _____
☐ _____

☐
_____
☐ Quantification Plan – Reporting vehicle

Appendix D

Executive Summary

<u>COMPANY NAME</u>

Full address and phone number

Prepared:
   by:

Pg. 1 of ____

Introduction to the company:

Company name is in the business of _____
…

The objectives of this plan is to *acquire funding* for the project _____ …

Company name has been in operations for …

Company name manufactures, sells, provides ….

1.
2…

Funding:

Company name is requesting $_____ to implement our project. This amount has been determined based on all requirements listed on page ____ in our main business plan. This amount has been verified and is included in our Financial Plan which is available upon request.

Management and Advisors:

Based on the experience and skills present in our

management team and .... _Company name_ is in a good position to accomplish our goals.

Director 1
Name:
Address:
Phone number:
Email:
-
-
-
Resume attached

Director 2
-
-

Risks:

As with any project certain possible risks have been identified. A chart has been produced based on our Risk Assessment & Contingency Plan. This chart shows that we are in a very good position ...

Insert risk chart here

CHRISTOPHER KAIZER

Financial Information:

<u>Company name</u> currently has revenue of … and assets of …

Financial information is available upon request. <u>Or</u> Financial information is attached.

If giving financial information you need to include name of bank and contact information of manager.

<u>Company name</u> holds a business account at ….

Supporting documentation:

Include names of supporting documents. Can include Charts and other condensed versions of the information you used to arrive at your assumptions.

That's it.

Pg. ___ of ___

11160269R00128

Made in the USA
Charleston, SC
03 February 2012

Greetings from TORONTO Canada

Greetings from TORONTO Canada

Greetings from Toronto Canada

Greetings from Toronto Canada

Greetings From TORONTO Canada

Greetings from Toronto Canada

Greetings from Toronto Canada

Greetings from TORONTO Canada

Greetings from TORONTO Canada

Greetings from TORONTO Canada

Greetings from TORONTO Canada

Greetings from TORONTO Canada

Greetings from TORONTO Canada

Greetings from Toronto Canada

Greetings from Toronto Canada

Greetings from TORONTO Canada

Greetings from Toronto Canada